KU-449-826

# TRACING YOUR ANCESTORS THROUGH FAMILY PHOTOGRAPHS

*A Complete Guide for
Family and Local Historians*

Jayne Shrimpton

Pen & Sword
**FAMILY HISTORY**

First published in Great Britain in 2014
PEN & SWORD FAMILY HISTORY
an imprint of
Pen & Sword Books Ltd
47 Church Street
Barnsley
South Yorkshire
S70 2AS

Copyright © Jayne Shrimpton 2014

ISBN 978 1 78159 280 9

The right of Jayne Shrimpton to be identified as Author of the Work
has been asserted by her in accordance with the Copyright,
Designs and Patents Act 1988.

A CIP catalogue record for this book is
available from the British Library.

All rights reserved. No part of this book may be reproduced or transmitted
in any form or by any means, electronic or mechanical including photocopying,
recording or by any information storage and retrieval system, without
permission from the Publisher in writing.

Typeset in Palatino and Optima by
CHIC GRAPHICS

Printed and bound in England by
CPI Group (UK), Croydon, CR0 4YY


Pen & Sword Books Ltd incorporates the imprints of Pen & Sword Archaeology,
Atlas, Aviation, Battleground, Discovery, Family History,  History, Maritime,
Military, Naval, Politics, Railways, Select, Social History, Transport, True Crime,
and Claymore Press, Frontline Books, Leo Cooper, Praetorian Press,
Remember When, Seaforth Publishing and Wharncliffe.

For a complete list of Pen & Sword titles please contact
PEN & SWORD BOOKS LTD
47 Church Street, Barnsley, South Yorkshire, S70 2AS, England
E-mail: enquiries@pen-and-sword.co.uk
Website: www.pen-and-sword.co.uk

C29 0000 0696 571

# TRACING YOUR ANCESTORS THROUGH FAMILY PHOTOGRAPHS

# FAMILY HISTORY FROM PEN & SWORD

FLINTSHIRE

SIR Y FFLINT

| C29 0000 0696 571 | |
| --- | --- |
| Askews & Holts | 07-Oct-2014 |
| 929.1072 | £14.99 |
| FL | |

# CONTENTS

# ACKNOWLEDGEMENTS

Many individuals have helped with the preparation of this book. I am indebted to colleagues, family and friends who have given freely of their time and expertise or have permitted photographs from their personal, group or professional collections to be featured. Special thanks are due to military expert Jon Mills and Ron Cosens of Photographers of Great Britain and Ireland 1840–1940/Victorian Image Collection.

* * * *

# PICTURE CREDITS

Fiona Adams 7, 30, 34, 48, 83–5, 104–5, 123, 150; Pat Brady 31, 42, 68, 81, 149; Agnes Burton 37, 62, 92; Patrick Davison 77, 101, 144; Claire Dulanty 39, 54, 56, 98, 103, 113, 148, 151; Julian Hargreaves 76, 79, 90, 112, 142; Mike Kostiuk (Family Tree Folk) 152; Simon Martin 29, 50, 60, 63, 67, 80, 86, 89; John Mills 114, 116, 120–1, 124–6, 129, 135, 139; Heather Redman 143; Richards Family 4; Ringmer History Study Group 2; Ann Thiessen 66, 82; Beryl Venn 3, 33, 44, 71, 75, 93, 102, 110, 117, 147; Victorian Image Collection 73, 91; Katharine Williams 6, 8, 26, 35–6, 38, 40, 45–7, 49, 58–9, 64–5, 69–70, 74, 78, 87–8, 94–5, 99, 106, 108–9, 115, 118, 122, 127–8, 130, 132–4, 136–8, 145. The remaining images are from the author's collection.

# INTRODUCTION

Early in 1839 the new 'invention' of photography was announced to the world by photographic pioneers in Britain and France. Within two years of this it was becoming possible for members of the public to have their photographs taken in one of the commercial portrait rooms being established in major cities, and twenty years later photography was opening up to a wide population. The new medium of photographic portraiture profoundly affected the way in which our ancestors viewed themselves and their contemporaries – and how others have seen them ever since. The surviving photographs handed down the generations that now form today's private picture archives provide family historians with an unrivalled opportunity not only to touch the personal items that were once handled and treasured by past family members, but to study their likenesses and gain a unique insight into their lives.

Old photographs have often been hoarded in attics, garages, cupboards and drawers but it is never too soon to resurrect and review these precious heirlooms. Whether our photograph collections comprise mainly twentieth-century snapshots or include formal Victorian studio portraits, these historical images need to be organised, examined carefully and researched in order to discover their origins and meaning. Very few family photographs date from before the 1850s, but even mid-nineteenth-century images can take us back six, seven or even eight generations of the family and may portray ancestors born in the eighteenth century. This book focuses on photographs dating from the 1840s up until the 1940s: this is not to suggest that later snapshots aren't important, but drawing a line at around 1950 ensures adequate coverage of the period that falls largely outside many researchers' living memory.

In the average family collection there will be photographs that are firmly identified or recognisable, and some that are not – enigmatic portraits of strangers staring back at us, encased in their archaic garments. They were all members of our family once, or were closely connected to ancestors and relatives, so the preservation of their images among the family memorabilia is significant, even if we don't yet fully understand why. Working with old images is different to consulting official documents and other factual written or printed records with which genealogists are familiar: photographs are expressions of reality but, being visual impressions, they may be open to a degree of interpretation. To those unused to examining pictures, making sense of unidentified photographs can seem daunting: we want to know all about them, and *now*, but sometimes the facts and stories surrounding images emerge gradually. Photographs contain a number of clues and only when all the evidence has been gathered and assimilated can we begin to assign them to their correct place in time and fully understand how they fit into the family's history.

*Tracing Your Ancestors Through Family Photographs* has been written through the eyes of a dress historian and picture specialist with many years' experience of professionally dating and analysing family and local history photographs. The book aims to explain the fundamentals of dating, examining and interpreting photographs, addressing the queries that commonly arise when family historians begin to study their inherited photographs, and suggesting ways of extending picture research so that no stone is left unturned. It is not essential to have access to a computer to discover more about old photographs, but with vast quantities of visual material and other relevant information now online it is a tremendous advantage to be able to conduct Internet searches, to consult photographic websites and also to be able to share and discuss digital images with others: investigations may be limited without resort to modern technology.

The first section of the book guides researchers in accurately dating their photographs: this is of paramount importance, an essential starting point when trying to identify unknown family members and conducting further picture research. Each chapter here explains a different photograph dating technique: all are widely recognised methods and can be used in conjunction with one another to assign a realistic time frame to undated photographs. Part Two explains how, having established a useful date range, we might delve deeper into our family photographs, study them more closely to see what else they reveal: for example, what occasion may have prompted ancestors and relatives to visit the photographer in their 'Sunday best' and what their images indicate about age and social status. We also look at the different types of copy pictures that might occur in a family photograph collection, how to date and analyse the contents of old albums and consider physical resemblance and other issues that emerge when comparing old photographs.

In Part Three we view photographs as primary historical sources – visual records that depict some of the key aspects of human life in the past, including weddings, the home, work, leisure pursuits and travel. A separate chapter considers the inextricable links between studying family and local history: family history is part of our wider heritage and so local sources can shed light on a family's past, and vice versa. We also focus closely on First and Second World War photographs, some of the most poignant images to survive in family collections, with particular emphasis on the Great War (1914–18), in recognition of the centenary that coincides with the publication date of this book. By 2014, many international, national, regional and local organisations will be hosting events and engaging in projects to commemorate the First World War, so there will be ample opportunity for researchers to celebrate, share and discover more about their own photographs and other personal mementoes of the conflict that changed everyone's lives. Finally, we look at how to care for old photographs, how to have them professionally conserved if necessary and ensure that we preserve these irreplaceable heirlooms in a suitable manner for the education and enjoyment of future generations.

*Part One*

# DATING FAMILY PHOTOGRAPHS

# Chapter 1

# RECOGNISING DIFFERENT TYPES OF PHOTOGRAPH

As commercial portrait photography progressed from its beginnings in the early 1840s, new photographic processes were developed, resulting in different types, or *formats*, of photograph. It isn't necessary for picture researchers to know a great deal about the technical aspects of photography, but it is very useful to be able to identify the various kinds of photographs that were created over the decades. Here we explain how to recognise different photographic formats from their physical characteristics and consider their period of production, their approximate cost and relative popularity. With an accurate historical framework and a basic social and economic context for the main types of photograph occurring in the family collection, we can begin to understand more about these images and, importantly, can form an approximate idea of when each one originated.

## Daguerreotypes, 1841–Early 1860s (Most Common Mid-1840s–Late 1850s)

Professional portrait photographs became available to the British public in 1841 when the first commercial studios were established in London and in other major cities. They produced *daguerreotype* portraits – high-quality photographic images struck directly onto a silvered copper plate (Fig. 1). Surviving daguerreotype photographs are recognisable from their highly polished, mirror-like surface, from the reversed image (as seen, for example, in the buttoning of garments) and from their tendency, when tilted at different angles, to fluctuate between a negative and a positive image. Daguerreotypes may be delicately coloured in places, as they were sometimes retouched by hand, using paint. They are often tarnished with a bluish tinge, especially around the edges, and the plate might also display fine scratches as the surface was easily damaged. Being vulnerable photographs, daguerreotypes were usually protected under a layer of glass and slotted into a frame suitable for hanging on the wall, or bound in a gilt frame and fitted into a neat folding case. Many cases were made of red leather-covered wood and opened on hinges like a book, with a padded red plush (cotton velvet) lining facing the picture inside.

**1. Daguerreotype, *c.* late 1840s–mid-1850s.** The earliest commercially produced portrait photograph was the daguerreotype, a luxury one-off portrait purchased mainly by wealthy ancestors. Daguerreotypes were rapidly superseded by new formats, becoming virtually obsolete by *c.* 1860.

Daguerreotypes were unique, one-off photographs and expensive portraits. Those taken by top-ranking photographers such as Antoine Claudet typically cost between £1 3s 6d and £1 13s 6d, while most photographers of the early 1840s charged around 1 guinea each. Such sums – considerably more than the average urban weekly wage – were comparable to the cost of commissioning a hand-painted portrait miniature, so early daguerreotype photographs were essentially the preserve of the wealthier classes: the landed gentry, members of the professions and successful businessmen and their families. In time prices lowered, particularly in the provinces, where cased daguerreotypes typically cost between 12s 6d and 14s by 1844, while increased commercial competition encouraged a continuing reduction in prices. However, daguerreotypes remained luxury items that ordinary working people could not afford: they also pre-date the major boom in portrait photography, so are now highly collectable artefacts but occur only rarely in today's family collections. Most surviving British examples date from between the mid-1840s and the late 1850s, for by the mid-1850s a new photographic format was becoming fashionable and would render the exclusive daguerreotype outmoded.

**Ambrotypes, *c.* 1852–90s (Studio Ambrotypes Common *c.* 1855–62)**
In 1851 a new photographic process using transparent glass plates was introduced. The *wet collodion* method was welcomed by portrait photographers,

although its commercial use was limited until 1855, when early patent and licence restrictions were effectively lifted. The glass-plate negative could be used to create positive prints, but most photographers adopted the method devised in 1852, which entailed converting the negative into an apparently positive photograph, by bleaching the image and blacking one side of the glass. The resulting glass photographs were called *collodion positives* in Britain, but were patented in the United States as *ambrotypes* and are now best known by this name. Ambrotype portraits resembled daguerreotypes in elegance, but were cheaper to produce, encouraging a significant rise in commercial photography during the mid to late 1850s. The first ambrotypes sold for around 10s 6d each but prices rapidly plummeted with the opening of more studios and increased commercial competition: by 1857 they could cost just 1s, this lowering further to 6d (plus 2d extra for a case) by 1858. It was the affordable ambrotype that began to open up the possibility of portrait photography to more of our ancestors (Fig. 2).

Surviving ambrotypes may potentially be confused with daguerreotypes as they, too, are one-off photographs – solid, three-dimensional objects. Many are reversed images, depending on which side of the glass was blackened: some

**2. Ambrotype, 1857.** Glass ambrotypes were less expensive than daguerreotypes and became fashionable from around the mid-1850s onwards. Mary Wickens of Upper Clayhill Farm, Ringmer, East Sussex (born in 1827), was photographed on her 30th birthday.

appear the right way round. The black backing was generally *shellac* (lacquer), occasionally velvet, and some ambrotypes show signs of deterioration, cracks or patches of clear glass appearing where the shellac has flaked away – a helpful identifying feature. Ambrotypes were often retouched by hand to add depth and render the portrait more life-like, so there may remain a pink blush on cheeks, bright gilding on buttons or jewellery and traces of colour on dress fabrics. Being fragile, the glass plate was usually protected by another layer of glass and mounted in a decorative surround of brass or cheaper pinchbeck. Some ambrotypes were sold uncased with a metal ring or loop of thread at the top for hanging the photograph; others were presented in hinged cases of leather or wood, papier mâché and leather cloth substitutes. Like cased daguerreotypes, a single ambrotype might face a pad of velvet or plush, although double ambrotypes also occur, the two photographs presented side by side inside the case. Late in 1854 a new moulded casing made from an early form of plastic was patented in the United States – the Union Case – and these were used in Britain from *c*. 1855 through to the mid-1870s.

Since ambrotypes were more affordable in their day than luxury daguerreotype portraits, they may represent ancestors from different social and occupational backgrounds, ranging from genteel ladies and gentlemen and teachers, to milliners, straw plaiters, post boys, police constables, tradesmen and gold prospectors. Most ambrotypes set in the photographer's studio originated within a short time period, between *c*. 1855 and the beginning of the 1860s; however, itinerant and outdoor photographers continued producing the glass photographs for much longer and examples taken in the open air may date from as late as the 1880s or even the 1890s.

### Cartes de Visite, c. 1859–1919 (Most Common 1861–c. 1906)
The brief fashion for studio ambrotypes is explained by the introduction of a revolutionary new photographic format, which would soon eclipse earlier portrait photographs. In 1854 a new process patented by Frenchman André Adolphe-Eugène Disdéri (1819–89) produced multiple identical photographic prints that were pasted onto card mounts. Measuring a neat 10cm x 6.5cm, or thereabouts, each card-mounted photograph was the size of a visiting card, and the format was named the *carte de visite* (Fig. 3). The *carte*, or *cdv*, arrived in Britain in around 1858. Initially a little slow to catch on, only a few British studios were producing *cartes* in 1859, but interest steadily grew and the August 1860 publication of John Mayall's *Royal Album*, a collection of *cartes de visite* portraits of the royal household, ensured their future. The album sold many copies but ultimately *cartes* were most desirable as individual photographs: the general public now wanted not only pictures of royalty and other 'celebrities' of the day, but also portrait *cartes* of themselves and their relatives. As demand soared during 1861, many more photographic studios

**3. *Carte de visite*, 1865.** The neat card-mounted photographic print known as the *carte de visite* brought portrait photography to a mass-population during the 1860s. For a few extra pence the image could be hand-coloured.

opened throughout Britain and by October *cartes de visite* were reportedly the most popular type of portrait. The year 1862 was the peak of commercial success, and sales remained high in 1863 before settling down to a steady output in 1864. The craze that seized Britain in the early 1860s was known as 'cartomania', as consumers avidly bought, collected, exchanged and gave away photographic cards on an unprecedented scale.

Unlike daguerreotypes and ambrotypes, both unique photographs, *cartes de visite* were mass-produced prints that conveniently allowed customers to buy multiple portraits. Cameras usually took eight *carte de visite* photographs simultaneously and several copies might be purchased at the initial sitting, although studios retained the negatives so that clients could order further copies later on. For those desiring a more picturesque image, the prints could be artistically hand-painted, for an additional fee, as seen in Fig. 3. In 1862 the average *carte de visite* cost around 1s 6d, but by 1864, as professional studios multiplied throughout the country and competition forced price cuts, some low-end photographers were charging just 5s for twelve copies. At these sorts of prices, many more ordinary working families could afford to visit the photographer and indeed by the mid-1860s it was becoming common for even our labouring ancestors to sit for a photographic portrait, to mark a special occasion in their lives. The convenient *carte de visite* print had brought photography to a wide population.

It is difficult to overstate the success and importance of the *carte de visite* photograph, which dominated Victorian portrait photography. It was the principal format of the 1860s and 1870s and remained popular throughout the 1880s, only facing significant competition during the 1890s from the larger cabinet print. Any of today's photograph collections dating back to the nineteenth century are likely to include *cartes de visite*, which are easy to identify from their standard, neat size. Early twentieth-century *cartes* may also survive, as they were still being produced in the early 1900s and, in much smaller numbers, until the First World War.

## Cabinet Prints, 1866–*c.* 1919 (Most Common Late 1870s–*c.* 1910)

As the initial rush on *cartes de visite* photographs slowed down, photographers welcomed any innovations that might boost the market further. In 1866 the cabinet photograph (also called the cabinet portrait, card or print) was introduced, another card-mounted photographic print but, measuring around 16.5cm x 11.5cm, over twice the size of the *carte de visite* (Fig. 4). Despite its active promotion, there was initially little interest in the new larger cabinet format, perhaps partly because the unit price was rather high at around 4s. However, demand increased during the 1870s and by the 1880s cabinet cards were becoming a popular choice, finally outselling the smaller *carte* during the 1890s. Cabinet prints, like *cartes*, were still being produced in the early

THE CABINET PORTRAIT.

VILLIERS & SONS. VS LLANDRINDOD WELLS,
PHOTOGRAPHERS ROYAL. & NEWPORT, MON.

**4. Cabinet print, mid-1870s.** The cabinet print or portrait measuring around 16.5cm x 11.5cm was introduced in 1866 but only became fashionable from around the mid-1870s onwards. It went on to dominate late-Victorian and Edwardian photography.

1900s and even into the 1910s, in dwindling numbers. Cabinet cards dominated the market for portrait photography in the late Victorian and Edwardian eras and a great many examples survive in family collections today.

## Unusual Card-Mounted Formats, 1860s–Early 1900s
Early variations on the successful *carte de visite* included the Diamond Cameo, introduced in 1864: this comprised an arrangement of four tiny portraits on a *carte*-sized mount, each displaying a different view of the sitter's face, although

these were never widely popular and few examples survive. Following the launch of the cabinet portrait in 1866, other photographic card formats were trialled. The Victoria, for example, was introduced into Britain from the United States in 1871, and was sized between the *carte* and the cabinet. Other new formats exceeded the cabinet, like the Boudoir (approximately 20.5cm x 13cm) and the Imperial (21.5cm x 16cm), both launched in 1875. Further novelties were promoted during the 1880s, for instance the Mignon (1883), smaller than the *carte* at around 2.5cm x 1.5cm. Other card formats appeared in the ensuing decades, but none attained anything like the popularity of the *carte de visite* and the cabinet print. Nonetheless, researchers should be aware of their existence as examples of these photographic prints may occasionally occur in family collections.

### Tintypes (Ferrotypes), Produced in Britain 1870s–c. 1950

The cheapest of all photographic portraits was the tintype, or *ferrotype*, an image struck directly onto an iron plate, using the wet collodion process (Fig. 5). The technique was patented in the United States in 1856 and was developed mainly for itinerant photographers, with all the operations taking place inside a special, multi-lensed camera. Some cameras could produce as many as thirty-six exposures on a plate, the plate being processed quickly, removed from the camera, cut up with scissors into separate tintypes and presented to the customer while still wet. Like daguerreotypes and ambrotypes, the pictures were unique, but they only cost a few pence each. Popular for many years in the United States, tintypes were scarcely recognised in Britain until 1872, when the first ferrotype studio opened in London's Regent Street. Despite the importation of instruction manuals and equipment and active publicity campaigns, tintypes were regarded by many British studio photographers as low-status, poor-quality images, although they were welcomed by outdoor photographers who produced on-the-spot photographic souvenirs at the seaside, fairgrounds and on the street. Upmarket photographers avoided the cheap novelties, although some high-street studios catering for the lower end of the market began to introduce ferrotypes during the mid–late 1870s in areas such as Bristol, London, Liverpool, Birmingham, Manchester, Glasgow and Edinburgh.

Most tintypes are fairly small in size – often no more than 6.5cm x 3.5cm – and by around 1880 a demand arose for tiny gem tintypes. The smallest commercially produced portrait, the so-called American Gem, was a diminutive postage-stamp-sized photograph which retailed at around 7½d for nine copies. If unmounted or unframed, tintypes are easily identified, as essentially they are photographs on a thin, sharp-edged piece of metal. The images tend to have a murky, metallic appearance and there may be very obvious signs of deterioration, such as rusting of the metal or flaking or

**5. Tintype, early 1890s.** Tintypes were cheap photographic images struck onto a thin piece of iron. Especially popular with outdoor photographers, in Britain they were produced mainly between the 1870s and 1940s. Typically unlabelled, the fashion clues suggest the early 1890s for this tintype.

bubbling of the photographic emulsion coating, as seen in Fig. 5. Other tintypes may be harder to recognise as, like daguerreotypes and ambrotypes, they were sometimes presented under a layer of glass and mounted in a gold-coloured frame. Some tintypes were inserted into standard *carte de visite* mounts or other cards, including mounts with an open aperture bordered by a decorative printed or embossed surround. Being easily cut to size, tiny gem tintypes were also ideal for fitting into jewellery, so they may be found, for example, in a locket or brooch that has survived as a family heirloom. If in doubt about whether a photograph is a tintype, a gentle magnet (like a fridge magnet) can be applied and will attract a tintype without causing damage, whereas it will not attract a daguerreotype, ambrotype or paper print.

A number of today's family picture archives include one or more tintypes. While tintypes may sometimes depict ancestors posing formally in a studio, often they were taken outdoors and portray their subjects in more casual settings, for example on the beach. The earliest tintypes in British family collections date from the 1870s onwards: many originated between the 1880s and the 1930s, although examples as late as the 1940s, even the early 1950s, are known.

### Portrait Postcards ('Real Photo Postcards'), c. 1902–40s

A new card-mounted photographic portrait emerged at the beginning of the twentieth century when studio photographers began to produce postcard photographs (Fig. 6). Picture postcards had been an authorised form of postal communication since the 1890s but initially the entire back of the card had been reserved for the address, so if posted, any message from the sender had to be written across the picture. However, in 1902 a new postcard design was introduced, with a line running down the centre of the reverse that offered separate spaces for the address and a short written message, thus preserving the image on the front. It was probably this convenient divided-back arrangement that first inspired commercial photographers to use postcards for portraits, producing 'real photo postcards', as they are sometimes called. These could be posted like any other postcard and some were, but often the card was kept chiefly for the image on the front. A few studios were producing postcard portraits as early as 1902 or 1903, although most surviving examples in family collections date from at least 1906 or 1907. By the end of the Edwardian era they had virtually eclipsed the traditional *cdv* and cabinet print and became the most common photographic format of the 1910s–40s, finally dying out after the Second World War.

Most photographic postcards measure a standard 14cm x 9cm, the size introduced for postcards in November 1899, although slight variations may occur. Visually the majority of formal studio postcard photographs look like any other professional portraits, posed according to contemporary convention in a fashionable setting, as discussed below in Chapter 4, although some were light-hearted or humorous and may occasionally exhibit novelty settings: for example their subjects may be 'flying' or 'driving' mock aeroplanes or cars. Popular with people from all walks of life and sometimes representing day-trip

**6. Postcard photograph, 1910.** Postcard mounts were first used by professional portrait photographers in 1902. Common from *c.* 1907 onwards, they became the most popular format of the early–mid-twentieth century.

or holiday souvenirs, postcards are today recognised as the most 'democratic' form of vintage photograph. Some professional outdoor photographers pictured local residents and street scenes on postcards, while even amateur photographers might have their snapshots printed onto postcard mounts.

Therefore, all private picture collections dating back to the early–mid-twentieth century will feature postcard photographs.

## Amateur Snapshots, Victorian Era–Present Day (Most Common 1910s onwards)

Amateur photography (as opposed to professional, commercial photography) was practised from the earliest days, although for many years it remained a genteel pastime for the prosperous classes who could afford the expensive, complex equipment and had the leisure time to experiment with the medium. Later, in the mid–late 1880s various innovations gave a significant boost to amateur photography. New ready-made dry photographic plates were faster and much more convenient to use than the cumbersome wet-plate method, while price reductions in photographic products made photography more affordable for middle-class hobbyists. In the United States, George Eastman (1854–1932) was also trialling gelatine-coated, paper-backed film for use in roll form, in a specially designed camera. In 1888 he launched the Kodak No. 1 camera, a relatively simple box camera loaded with a 100-exposure roll of film that was sent back to the Eastman factory when finished, reloaded and returned to the customer while the first roll was processed. Although traditional glass plates were still used by professionals and serious amateurs for many more years, for the casual 'snapshooter', taking photographs for pleasure no longer required advanced technical skills, artistic ability or complicated apparatus. Amateur snapshot photography continued to gain momentum in the early twentieth century. In 1900 the user-friendly film-loaded Kodak Box Brownie camera was introduced, an affordable model still popular in the 1940s. Meanwhile, during the 1910s new cameras were also introduced, such as the Kodak Vest Pocket Camera, launched in 1912. After the First World War the box or folding camera became a familiar gadget in many homes: the taking of casual snapshots to record both special occasions and everyday scenes was becoming a regular part of family life (Fig. 7).

The survival of snapshot photographs in today's family collections closely reflects the progress of amateur photography, as outlined above. Early photographs taken by affluent ancestors in the mid-nineteenth century, as exemplified by Fig. 97, are rare, and any surviving Victorian snapshots are most likely to date from the later 1880s or 1890s, when the middle classes became more involved in photography (Figs 68 and 149). The vast majority of casual snapshots in today's family archives date from the twentieth century, some originating in the early 1900s, although many more date from the mid–late 1910s onwards: from then on amateur snapshots increasingly dominate our photograph collections. Many twentieth-century snapshots are contact prints that relate directly to the size of the film that was used. The first Box Brownie cameras produced 5.7cm square prints, while the No. 2 Brownie camera, launched in 1901, gave larger (5.7cm x 8.3cm) snapshots – a size that remained popular for over fifty years. The 1912 Kodak Vest Pocket camera produced pictures of 6.4cm x 4.2cm. Postcard-style snapshots were

**7. Amateur snapshot, early 1920s.** Although affluent Victorian ancestors may have been keen amateur photographers, most snapshots in family collections date from at least the 1910s, when home photography became more widespread.

also common in the early twentieth century, these usually measuring 8.3cm x 14cm, while other larger prints became more common between the wars, especially during the 1930s. The size of family snapshots can therefore offer a rough dating guide, although we can expect to determine a closer time frame using other photograph dating methods.

## Early Twentieth-Century Card-Mounted Studio Photographs

Despite the growing popularity of amateur photography in the early twentieth century, the professional portrait survived and was still considered a superior product: studios continued producing traditional *cdvs* and cabinet prints until the 1910s, as well as the new postcard photograph. However, some photographs of the new century don't fit into any of those familiar formats: the professional photographer's repertoire also included larger mounted prints, quarter plate (10.2cm x 12.7cm) being a standard size, although larger pictures were always possible and were particularly well suited to group scenes. Very stout matt card in sober or soft colours such as cream, beige, grey, brown and

**8. Card-mounted studio portrait, *c.* early 1910s.** Another common format of the early–mid-twentieth century was the print pasted onto or framed by a sturdy card mount with a wide border. Popular card colours included cream, beige, grey, green and brown.

dusty green was used for presenting these photographs. Mounts were typically much larger than the photographic print and the wide frame offered scope for subtle detailing: for example, a series of borders or a decorative surround might be pressed into the card, outlining the picture (Fig. 8). This style continued after the First World War and throughout the inter-war era, although as photographic developing papers became sturdier, the need for a robust mount declined and sometimes photographs were instead slipped into a folding card. By the late 1910s the fold-over card was becoming popular: this might have pre-cut slots in the back section for containing the photograph, while the front folded over, protecting the image. Plain or coloured, embossed or printed with a design or logo, the folding card method of presenting photographs remained popular throughout much of the twentieth century (Fig. 9).

**9. Folding card photograph by Veale & Co. of Bristol, 1940s.** Studio photographs presented in a folding card were popular from the 1910s onwards, remaining common throughout the twentieth century.

# Chapter 2

# INVESTIGATING PHOTOGRAPHERS AND STUDIOS

**Photographer Information**

Family photographs taken in a professional studio may bear the name and studio address of the photographer: this is important historical evidence. Studio details may be embossed on the case lid of daguerreotype and ambrotype photographs or printed on a label attached to the back, although, frustratingly, information is often absent from these one-off metal and glass plates, and also from tintypes. Fortunately, however, most photographs in the family collection are card-mounted photographic prints and the mounts provided commercial photographers with an ideal opportunity to identify their work and advertise their business. With *cartes de visite*, cabinet prints and non-standard portraits, sometimes the name and studio address were printed neatly on the front, below the picture, but the reverse offered a larger space, which was used to publicise one or more studios, to elaborate on photographic services such as enlargements and copies, and to promote any other features likely to impress clients, such as royal patronage or prestigious photographic awards. The new twentieth-century formats tended to be less explicit in their printed details: postcards often omit the photographer, although sometimes a studio name and address were printed or ink-stamped on the back, as seen in Figs 6 and 25. Usually the stout card mounts used for larger early twentieth-century prints and smaller folding cards bear the studio name in modest lettering (Figs 8 and 9).

When studio details occur on an old photograph, they provide a firm geographical location and also offer another potential method of dating the picture. The town or city suggests the likely place of residence for the ancestor(s) represented in the portrait, as clients usually visited a studio close to home, either in the town or city in which they lived or in their nearest urban centre if their village or hamlet had no resident photographer. There are some exceptions to this general principle: for instance, an ancestor who left home to study or work elsewhere may have visited a local photographer's studio, or family members may have had a souvenir photograph taken while on a day trip to the seaside or a fashionable tourist resort. Of course, the various journeys made by past family members were not always recorded, although we may have formed some idea of their usual movements. Ultimately, the geographical location of a studio portrait always confirms that its subjects were in that area at some point in time: this is important to bear in mind when considering possible candidates for an unidentified photograph. The locations of studio photographs can also assist wider research, by revealing ancestors' whereabouts in the years between census dates.

Naturally, photographers specified on their mounts not only the town or city in which they operated, but also the building name or number and the street. These details can be very useful when attempting to date a photograph, as discovering when a named photographer worked at the stated address indicates the time period within which it must have been taken (with the occasional exception of copy prints – dealt with in Chapter 7). Some photographers may have run a particular studio for just a few years, and clearly this narrows down the date range for any photographs taken at that address; however, if he or she operated the same studio for many years, then only a broad circa date is possible for photographs originating there and a closer time frame will need to be ascertained using other photograph dating methods. Photographers who expanded their business generally lost little time in having their card mounts reprinted to include details of additional branches. When two or more studio addresses are specified on a card mount, as seen, for example, in Figs 13, 19, 20 and 22, it is necessary to determine when both, or all of them were operating simultaneously. Some branches within a chain did not survive for very long, so the period of multiple studios may have spanned only a few years: this can help to determine a fairly precise date range for a photograph.

## Researching Photographers and Studios

Investigating a nineteenth- or early twentieth-century studio named on a photograph may be a lengthy process or can be surprisingly easy, depending upon whether or not accurate data has already been gathered and publicised in printed works or online. Photographic history generates significant interest and some old photographs, besides being family heirlooms, are collectable items, so a great deal of information has been compiled about past photographers and their operations, especially if they were well known in their day. For example, major public organisations that collect historic photographs, like the National Portrait Gallery, London, focus on eminent society photographers such as Alexander Bassano (1829–1913), James Lafayette (1853–1923) and famous studios like Hills and Saunders (established in 1852 and still operational today). Renowned photographers patronised by royalty and the social elite may possibly have photographed affluent and well-connected ancestors (see, for example, Fig. 86): if so, researchers will find much written about them and their activities in books, gallery and exhibition catalogues and in online sources.

In practice, relatively few family historians have ancestors who moved in high society a century or more ago and so most will be investigating names from among the many thousands of commercial photographers who ran regular high-street studios. Even at the middle and lower ends of the market, professional studio photography could be fairly lucrative but it was highly competitive. Photographers came from all walks of life and occupational backgrounds: some practised photography as a sideline alongside their main trade, or tried to become established as a photographer but struggled and relocated frequently, or eventually resorted to another line of work. The most transient operators left little tangible evidence of their activities, which can make it hard to discover much about them and their operational dates. However, photographers who remained in business for a significant period were recorded on census returns and probably advertised in local trade

**10.** *Carte de visite* **by Thos Shrimpton & Son of Oxford, *c.* 1880s.** Since photography was a popular occupation in the mid–late nineteenth and early twentieth centuries, we may have ancestors who ran professional studios. Their businesses can be researched using the usual photographer sources.

18

directories and newspapers, making it possible to trace their operations over time as they expanded into additional premises, joined up with new working partners or moved between different addresses.

Sometimes it may be necessary to consult original sources – census returns, trade directories and newspapers – to find references to a photographer named on a photograph. Considering the chronology of commercial photography, the first significant census return is 1851, while the returns for 1861 onwards are the most relevant for tracing photographers. Advertisements in local newspapers may be found online at the British Newspaper Archive: www.britishnewspaperarchive.co.uk. Business details may appear in the selected trade directories that are free to view at www.historicaldirectories.org. If using these sources, it is important to understand the nature of the data, its scope and, especially, its limitations: census returns will only reveal a photographer's location every ten years and, while trade directories and newspaper notices are useful, not all photographic studios advertised regularly in the press, so the years of any advertisements found may not necessarily reveal the full period of their operation at a given address. As with any kind of genealogical research, remember to consult local sources of information: district libraries, record offices and archives are likely to hold material relating to photographers once operating in their geographical area, although records do vary. A number of local organisations have published printed guides to the work of past photographers in their city or county, including their recorded operational dates. Some of the main publications are listed in the Sources section at the end of the book.

## Online Resources

The Internet is an invaluable tool when investigating past photographers and online research can produce reasonably accurate data for a given studio. A simple Google search for the photographer's name and address (try different search terms) should reveal any online references to the studio: results will, inevitably, vary and some links will be more useful than others, but with luck it may transpire that detailed research has already been conducted into the photographer under investigation and that his or her address and operative dates are recorded on a photography website for others to view. Currently, there exists no freely searchable comprehensive directory of nineteenth- and early twentieth-century British commercial photographers, and there are no known plans to undertake such a vast project; however, several important online photographer indexes and databases have been compiled by various institutions, regional organisations, local and family historians and independent photograph collectors and experts. Most of these data sets cover studios from a specific geographical area – usually a city or county – and provide A–Z photographer listings with dates of operation at each address.

Some also include additional biographical details about selected photographers and even examples of their photographs, with which researchers can compare their own family photographs. If using indexes and databases compiled by others, again be aware of the limitations of the information, which has usually been collected from census returns, trade directories and newspaper advertisements. Some only use certain sources and therefore do not claim to supply complete studio operational dates; where compilers cite the exact sources that they have used in their research, this allows viewers to judge their scope and reliability and decide whether further investigations are needed.

The principal searchable online indexes in existence at time of writing are listed in the Sources section of this book, but since Internet data is constantly being extended and updated, it is worth conducting regular searches for photographers named on family photographs. In general, databases offer a convenient short cut to researching early photographic studios: if the photographer under investigation is covered in an Internet listing, the dates provided should at least offer an approximate guide as to when he or she was in business. However, studio data for some areas of Britain has not yet been compiled or made widely available online. If a particular photographer cannot be found anywhere on the Internet and primary research using the original census returns and trade advertisements is not viable, there are a few specialist commercial websites that will provide British photographer data, including dates and details of photographers who are not always recorded elsewhere: these private services, which request a small fee, are also listed in the Sources section.

## Photographer Ancestors

Finally, while researching photographers, we should remember that a significant number of us will have ancestors – male or female – who were personally involved in the commercial photography business. They may have run a studio or studios in their own name (Fig. 10), perhaps travelled between different locations as an itinerant practitioner, or worked as an assistant at another photographer's studio. If they operated under their own name, their business dates and activities can be researched in much the same way as those of other photographers. A recommended guide to investigating past photographers in the family is *My Ancestor was a Studio Photographer* by Robert Pols (Society of Genealogists, 2011).

# Chapter 3

# DATING PROFESSIONAL
# PHOTOGRAPHIC CARD MOUNTS

As we saw in Chapter 1, *cartes de visite*, cabinet prints and less common professional card-mounted Victorian and Edwardian photographs differ in their dimensions: indeed, it is their size that denotes their format. These photographic mounts may also display distinct variations in the shape of their corners, the thickness of the card, the colour of the mount and the design on the reverse – physical features that changed significantly over the years, following fashion. The mounts used by a particular photographer may not always have represented the very latest style available, especially if he or she needed to finish using existing stocks before ordering new supplies, but in practice it was rare for active photographers to use very old card mounts. Therefore learning to recognise the card-mount characteristics associated with different decades helps with dating old photographs as objects – a technique that works well in conjunction with other photograph dating methods such as

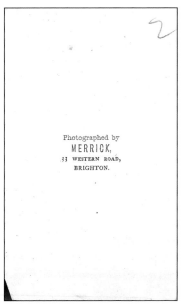

Photographed by
MERRICK,
33 WESTERN ROAD,
BRIGHTON.

**11. *Carte de visite*, early 1860s.** The earliest *cdv* mounts dating from the early–mid-1860s were very plain and usually bore a neat design centred on the card. Throughout the 1860s and for most of the 1870s corners were square.

**12. Carte de visite, mid-1860s–mid-1870s.** Mounts became more detailed as the 1860s advanced and often mention the negative and availability of copies by around mid-decade. The ribbon banner and filigree scrollwork were popular forms of ornamentation in the later 1860s/early 1870s.

**13. *Carte de visite*, late 1860s onwards.** Some mounts were rather elaborate by the later 1860s and began to mention medals won by the photographer. The years of any awards offer a firm *post quem* date.

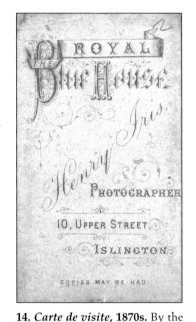

*15. Carte de visite,* **1870s.** During the 1870s coloured card mounts became fashionable, and the golden-yellow shade of this card was most popular during the 1870s and 1880s. The ribbon banner and heraldic shield were common 1870s devices.

*14. Carte de visite,* **1870s.** By the 1870s, the printed details sometimes spread across the entire mount and several different font styles were common. Ornate capital letters and slanting text were new features of the decade.

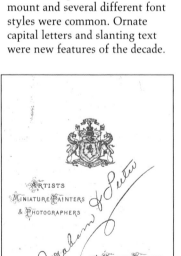

*16. Carte de visite,* **1870s.** This mount combines the popular 1870s features of slanting text (generally used for the photographer's name) and heraldic motif. This example is relatively restrained.

investigating the studio dates and dating the visual image. The remainder of this chapter outlines the physical features to look out for, with an explanation of their periods of popularity. The illustrations of mount reverse views demonstrate just some of the many different examples that may occur in family collections, although this is not a comprehensive guide: further examples of printed designs are displayed on a number of photographic websites, some of which are included in the Sources section.

## Card Thickness, Corner Shapes and Flyleaves

The earliest *cartes de visite* always have square corners, as seen in Figs 11–16, and the card is relatively thin and flexible, bending easily, like a playing card. The square-cornered shape prevailed from the time of the first *cdvs* until the mid-1870s: at around that point rounded corners began to appear on *cartes* and cabinet prints, becoming increasingly common during the 1880s. Mounts from the mid-1880s through to the early twentieth century usually have round corners, although square corners re-appeared occasionally at later dates, presenting exceptions to the rule.

The card used for mounts by the late nineteenth century was generally noticeably thicker and sturdier than that of earlier mounts, a development that encouraged bevelled edges and their finishing in silver or gold. In the 1880s and 1890s some photographs were also protected by a flyleaf – a covering of fine tissue pasted along the upper edge of the back of the card and folded over the front of the photograph. Usually, the tissue itself has not survived, but a narrow strip of tissue or evidence of glue along the top edge of the reverse may remain, offering another dating clue (Fig. 21).

## Mount Colours

Early *cdv* mounts dating from the 1860s were usually light in colour – ivory, off-white, cream and champagne (Figs 11–13). These neutral tones continued into the 1870s and beyond, although by the turn of the 1870s a vogue was emerging for coloured card mounts. Sugar pink (used for both male and female subjects) was popular for many years between the end of the 1860s and the early 1890s (Figs 4 and 17); common also during the 1870s and 1880s were bright golden yellow-coloured mounts (Figs 10 and 15), while a rarer shade was turquoise blue. Meanwhile, by the mid-1880s there was developing a taste for richer, darker colours: bright red-coloured mounts enjoyed a brief vogue in the later 1880s and early 1890s, while the most popular of the stronger shades were bottle green and black. Dark green, black and, less commonly, chocolate brown and maroon were all fashionable between *c.* 1884 and 1905 – a twenty-odd-year period that helps to pinpoint late-Victorian and early Edwardian photographs (Figs 30, 40 and 74). Co-existing with the fashion for dark-coloured mounts was a trend towards strong creams, apricots and beiges during the late 1880s and throughout the 1890s (Figs 19 and 20). Finally, card mounts in various shades of grey, from pale silver-grey through middling tones to dark slate grey, were common during the 1890s and early 1900s, being used frequently around the turn of the century (Figs 21–3, 37 and 101).

## Printed Mount Designs

*Cartes* and cabinet photographs were occasionally left completely blank on the back: this was common with dark-coloured mounts as these required gold or silver lettering, which was expensive. However, as we saw in Chapter 2, the reverse of most *cdvs* and cabinet portraits was printed with the name, address and other business details pertaining to the studio. Over the years more complex font styles and more elaborate decorative motifs were introduced, so the backs of card mounts became increasingly ornate – often works of art in their own right. A few printing companies specialised in supplying card mounts to commercial photographers: they offered mounts in a range of designs fashionable at any given time, to which individual studio details were added; hence photographers operating at opposite ends of the country might well choose the same mount designs, only their personal business information differing. Very occasionally a photographer favoured a unique mount design of local origin and, admittedly, these can be hard to identify and date. However, most card mounts surviving in family photograph collections bear generic designs that reflect the stylistic trends of their day: learning how to recognise these helps to narrow the potentially wide date range of *cdvs*, cabinet prints and similar card-mounted photographs.

The earliest *cartes de visite* produced in 1859/60 and during the next few years were very neatly printed (or occasionally ink-stamped) with the photographer's name and address in small lettering, the details usually presented in the centre of the mount (Fig. 11): the only additional markings were a crown or royal coat of arms if the studio could claim royal patronage. These simple early mount designs were current for just a few years: from around the mid-1860s onwards the text began to expand outwards across the card, and at the same time a line mentioning the availability of copies or duplicates was often added below the central design or at the bottom of the mount, as seen in Fig. 12 and later mounts. During the mid–late 1860s additional design features began to appear, especially delicate filigree scrollwork and ribbon-like banners (Fig. 12), these devices continuing throughout the 1870s, in a more prominent manner (Fig. 14).

In general, during the 1870s a greater variety of mount designs were produced. The inclusion of three or four different text fonts became a common feature, while heraldic-style crests and coats of arms were especially popular (Figs 12, 15 and 16). Medals or medallions announcing photography exhibitions or competition prizes also became more common: naturally, the

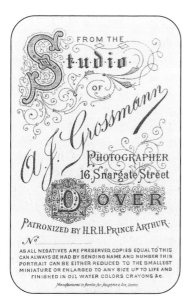

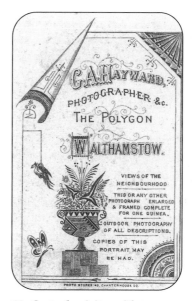

**17.** *Carte de visite,* **late 1870s–early 1890s.** Mount designs became denser over time, versions of this style with ornate capital letter and filigree scrollwork remaining popular for at least fifteen years. Pink card was fashionable *c.* 1870–early 1890s; rounded corners became common during the 1880s.

**18.** *Carte de visite,* **mid-1880s–mid-1890s.** Pictures began to appear on mounts during the 1880s, including rockets, urns, fans, birds and butterflies, all popular motifs between the early 1880s and later 1890s. This particular design – one of many variants – was used *c.* mid-1880s–mid-1890s.

year of any awards or exhibitions provides a firm *post quem* date for the photograph, as demonstrated in Fig. 13. Printed details became increasingly ornate, occupying more space on the reverse of the card. A typical late-1870s style that continued throughout the 1880s and turn of the 1890s displayed the studio name sprawled diagonally across the mount, bordered by ornate filigree work, the text embellished with a large highly decorated capital letter (Figs 10, 14 and 17). Another style seen mainly during the 1880s and early 1890s was the card with an elaborate border, the text and any other design features contained within (Fig. 20).

Following late-nineteenth-century aesthetic taste, mount designs of the 1880s and 1890s were highly complex, flamboyant lettering and expansive decoration usually filling the entire back of the mount (Figs 10 and 17–22). A characteristic of some late-Victorian mounts is the active promotion of the

**19. Cabinet, mid-1880s–late 1890s.** Figural designs were fashionable from around the mid-1880s until the late 1890s, chiefly classically dressed ladies, cherubs and fairies. Note the reference to artist here, typical of 1880s/1890s mounts.

**20.** *Carte de visite*, **mid-1880s–late 1890s.** During the 1880s and 1890s mounts sometimes have a border – plain or ornate – framing the printed information within. The artist's palette seen top left was a popular motif, this particular card design dating from the mid-1880s–late 1890s.

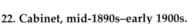

**21. Cabinet, late 1880s–late 1890s.** This popular design was used by many different photographers after the mid-1880s and during the 1890s. Traces of the flyleaf that once folded over the front of the picture confirm the late-Victorian date.

**22. Cabinet, mid-1890s–early 1900s.** Often 1890s and early 1900s mounts were grey in colour, as seen here. This example shows the more modern font style and shaded effects fashionable around the turn of the century, the printed details often dark blue or red/brown, as here.

photographers' artistic skills, the mention of 'Artist', 'Art photographer' or similar terms reflecting the concern of professional photographers to emphasise their superior status in the face of growing competition from amateur hobbyists (Fig. 19). Reinforcing the artistic theme, many mounts from the early 1880s through to the mid–late 1890s incorporate pictures: popular pictorial subjects were artists' easels, paint palettes, photographers' camera equipment (Fig. 19) and scenes depicting swimming or flying water birds among reeds or bamboo (Fig. 21). Also common during this period were exotic designs displaying blossom-laden branches, rockets, fans and parasols, expressing the contemporary vogue for Japanese or oriental imagery (Fig. 18). Classically draped female figures, cherubs and fairies may also occur on mounts of the mid-1880s through to the later 1890s (Fig. 19).

In the late 1890s mounts began to shed some of their more exuberant decoration and around the turn of century may appear more 'modern', almost streamlined in effect. Font styles are usually plainer, the lettering sometimes displaying shaded effects, while angular shapes begin to appear, alongside sunburst effects, small bunches of flowers and other botanical motifs (Fig. 22). Late *carte de visites* and cabinet prints dating from the Edwardian and pre-First World War era may be relatively simple, focusing mainly on the photographer's studio details and perhaps incorporating a monogram (Fig. 23).

## Postcard Backs

Many twentieth-century family photographs will be postcards. The above card-mount dating techniques will not apply to postcard mounts, but postcards may be broadly dated according to their own characteristics. For example, if a postcard was actually sent through the post and the postmark is legible, the date of postage is likely to be fairly close to the year of the picture. If the postmark cannot be read, then the postage stamp will at least show the head of the reigning monarch at the time it was sent: Edward VII ascended the throne in 1901, George V in 1910, Edward VIII in 1935, George VI in 1936 and Elizabeth II in 1952. The image of the king or queen and the monetary value of the postage stamp offer combined clues which should help to narrow the date range of a mailed postcard (Fig. 24). The inland postal rate for postcards was ½*d* until June 1918 and from then, until June 1921, it remained at 1*d*. From then the cost rose to 1½*d*, but dropped again in May 1922 to 1*d*.

Many surviving portrait postcards were not posted, although they may still offer helpful clues. The empty stamp box in the top right-hand corner can sometimes be dated approximately from its style – perhaps a decorative motif or manufacturer's name or initial. A useful online guide to identifying and approximately dating stamp boxes can be found, along with other information about 'real photo postcards', at www.playle.com/realphoto/photoall.php.

Otherwise, unmarked postcards can sometimes be broadly dated from the arrangement and nature of the printed wording on the back. As mentioned in Chapter 1, the divided back confirms a date of at least 1902, while the carefully worded explanation 'For Inland Postage ONLY, this space may now be used for communication' was common for several years following the introduction of the new style: cards bearing these instructions can roughly be dated to between 1902 and about 1910 (Fig. 25). The printed wording on postcards varied slightly, but by the 1910s it was generally fairly simple, often reduced to 'Correspondence' on one side of the dividing line and 'Address' or 'Name and address' on the other.

**23. Cabinet, early 1900s.** Late *cdvs* and cabinet cards of the Edwardian era were often coloured grey. Designs were becoming plainer and the studio name was often expressed in slanting font. A monogram was common at this time.

**24. Postcard, June 1918–1935.** When postcards have been posted, the stamp provides an extra clue. This postage stamp depicts King George V (1910–35), the 1*d* value confirming a date of at least June 1918, but not June 1921–May 1922, when postage temporarily rose to 1½*d*.

**25. Postcard, *c.* 1902–10.** Postcards were popular for over forty years but often their style or printed details can narrow the date. These detailed instructions suggest an early date of *c.* 1902–10.

# Chapter 4

# DATING THE VISUAL IMAGE: STUDIO PORTRAITS AND OUTDOOR SCENES

Having examined photographic formats, photographer details and card-mount styles in the previous chapters, we now turn to the photographic image itself. While the methods outlined earlier all help with photograph dating, we should also consider the clues contained within the picture: by scrutinising the many visual elements of a scene, it is possible to estimate approximately when our forebears were photographed. In this chapter we concentrate on the pose and presentation – or *composition* – of the subject(s), and their surroundings, before looking more specifically at the evidence of dress in Chapter 5.

## Studio Portraits

Most Victorian and Edwardian photographs in today's family picture collections were taken by commercial photographers; so, too, were some more recent photographs, when our relatives desired a superior portrait. The majority of professional photographs originated in the studio and portray their subjects in an artificial environment. Studio sets can sometimes look rather like a theatrical stage as they may display a painted backcloth and used various 'props' to create a three-dimensional effect. Drapes, painted architectural features, fake windows, pieces of solid furniture and other moveable indoor accessories such as plant stands produced an idealised drawing room setting, while rocks, greenery, fences, gates and pergolas positioned against rustic scenery suggested a picturesque outdoor location. Studios kept special accessories to create a genteel, respectable ambience: quality toys such as dolls, spinning tops and musical instruments were provided for children, while adults often held a book, album or letter, implying literacy at a time when not everyone could read. Personal items could be brought along for photograph sittings, such as a child's favourite toy or a sporting ancestor's tennis racquet, but articles from home were only welcomed if they carried positive associations and helped to enhance the portrait.

When a client entered the studio, the photographer took control, composing them in a suitable manner, positioning the angle of their head, stance and placing of the legs, arms and feet to best advantage and suggesting an appropriate facial expression. Victorian ancestors were not generally inclined to grin cheerfully for the camera, but equally they did not wish to appear dull and wooden, so together client and photographer aimed for a 'pleasing expression' – one of dignity, pensiveness or intelligent seriousness. Until the 1880s, when faster dry photographic plates came into common use, thereby reducing the exposure time needed for the photograph, posing stands were sometimes used to help sitters maintain their pose: some were free-standing, while others were attached to chairs, and some involved uncomfortable head clamps. Women's full skirts covered the bases of stands effectively, although close inspection of men's and children's portraits may sometimes reveal a stand behind the feet.

Commercial photography studios usually took up to four different poses at the time of the sitting: once printed, they were shown to the customer who could then select which portrait(s) they wished to have mounted and to purchase. The resulting pictures reflected not only the client's personal choice, but also expressed the photographer's skills and the photographic conventions of the era – current ideas about composition and prevailing tastes in backdrops, furniture and other props. Since studio fashions changed significantly over the years, recognising the key stylistic features of different periods helps to narrow down the time frame of individual photographs.

## Dating the Composition and Setting
In the daguerreotypes and ambrotypes of the 1840s and 1850s, single figures are generally depicted close-up in a half-length or short three-quarter length composition. Usually, they are seated on a chair facing directly forward or slightly turned, with one elbow resting on an adjacent table. There may be a hint of background detail, occasionally a painted backcloth, and sometimes an elaborate cloth covers the table, but the main focus is on the subject (Figs 1, 2 and 26). Photographing several people at once in the studio presented a technical challenge in the mid-nineteenth century, so most early photographs portray just one or two people, rarely more than three. Over time larger groups became more common: to photograph two or more subjects together in the studio, the photographer had to move back, so several figures usually appear in full-length or long three-quarter length, whatever the period, as seen in Figs 31 and 44.

Some photographers continued using the early, close-up composition at the beginning of the 1860s, but when card-mounted *cdvs* became popular, a new visual image evolved. Typical *cartes* of the 1860s depict single subjects posing full-length – doll-like figures standing or sitting in what was usually a mock drawing room interior (Figs 3, 27, 41 and 50). Often a curtain is draped to one side and there are one or two pieces of solid furniture, perhaps an

**26. Ambrotype, mid–late 1850s.** In daguerreotypes and ambrotypes of the 1840s and 1850s, subjects were usually photographed close-up, seated at a table in a half- or short three-quarter-length pose.

architectural column or plinth, or a table and/or a chair. Usually, standing subjects support themselves, hand resting on a table top, chair or pedestal, although older ancestors in particular might be seated. With an expanse of room on display in these early *carte de visite* photographs, we often notice patterned flooring and a stretch of wainscot or skirting board. Sometimes there is a decorative backcloth, perhaps a painted window, door or archway opening onto a *trompe l'oeil* landscape beyond. Artistic studios were also experimenting with 'outdoor' settings by the later 1860s (Fig. 29): these became more common in the following decades.

The convention for photographing studio clients as whole-length figures drifted over into the early 1870s and indeed full-length studio portraits may theoretically date from any period: some customers evidently preferred this type of composition, perhaps because it displayed their fashionable dress and

**27. *Carte de visite*, *c*. 1860–5.** A typical early *cdv* from the 1860s, this shows the subject posing full-length in a mock drawing room interior, with curtain draped to one side and pieces of furniture.

**28. *Carte de visite, c.* 1870.** During the 1870s photographers began to move in towards their subject and for the next twenty to thirty years, many portraits were three-quarter-length compositions. Backgrounds were often blank but furniture became more prominent.

accessories to best effect. However, by the turn of the 1870s, the predominant trend was for the camera to move in closer towards its subject, taking three-quarter length views in which the lower legs and feet were not pictured: this composition was very common for single portraits throughout the 1870s and 1880s and often helps with identifying photographs from those decades (Figs 28, 42, 72, 76 and 79). Three-quarter length subjects might be seated, perhaps at a table or leaning against the back of a chair: otherwise they stand, partially turned towards the camera or in profile. Little background detail is visible in these close-up photographs, the room behind the subject usually blank or sketchily depicted. However, furniture in the foreground becomes more prominent and we begin to notice familiar styles, such as the velvet, padded seat ornamented with tassels or fringing, typical of the 1870s and 1880s (Figs 42, 76 and 79).

Over time more diverse studio sets and scenery were used by commercial photographers. From the late 1860s onwards, and especially during the 1870s

**29.** *Carte de visite, c. 1867.* This shows the typical full-length pose of the 1860s. Weston & Son were prestigious, artistic photographers who were experimenting with elaborate painted backcloths and rustic props, ambitious outdoor settings at an early date.

and 1880s, there was a growing vogue for carefully contrived, naturalistic-looking 'outdoor' settings. Some sets evoked a pastoral scene, by means of a painted backcloth depicting a distant view or a wooded glade, while in the foreground rustic bark-covered fences, gates and stiles became fashionable, softened by imitation grass, ferns and leaves – all moveable studio props, sometimes enhanced by further painted vegetation (Figs 29 and 53).

By the 1880s, photographers operating in Victorian seaside resorts popular with holidaymakers and day-trippers often favoured marine themes: these might include mastheads, ships' decking, ropes, rocks and painted backcloths depicting the sea, harbour or beach (Fig. 30). Meanwhile, an accessory first introduced during the 1880s for interior settings, and therefore providing a

**30. Cabinet card, late 1880s.** Photographers operating seaside studios often contrived nautical-themed sets, with painted backcloths depicting sea or harbour and rocks or a ship in the foreground.

**31. *Carte de visite*, early–mid 1880s.** Groups of people were usually composed in full-length as the photographer moved back to fit everyone in the frame. The shaggy rug seen here first appeared in the 1880s, a prop that offers a helpful dating clue.

helpful *post quem* dating clue, is the shaggy fur-like rug or throw: spread on the floor or draped over a chair, this became a fashionable studio accessory from the 1880s onwards (Fig. 31).

Three-quarter length compositions continued into the 1890s, a long three-quarter length pose being popular (Figs 53 and 74). In these and in full-length group compositions, background scenery was more prominent and we may notice plant stands bearing potted palms, ferns and aspidistras and painted backcloths depicting palms, ferns and other large-leafed foliage, expressing the late-Victorian craze for exotic plant varieties (Figs 53, 71 and 74). However, even more typical of this decade was the head and shoulders *vignette* portrait in which the central image fades away around the edges into a blank background (Figs 32, 40 and 87). This composition, providing a very close-up view of the subject, was in vogue broadly between the late 1880s and beginning of the 1900s but was most characteristic of the 1890s.

**32. Cabinet card, mid-1890s.** The head and shoulders vignette portrait, whereby the image faded out around the edges, was used late 1880s–early 1900s, but was especially popular during the 1890s.

**33. Postcard, *c.* 1902–5.** Head and shoulders or short half-length portraits were sometimes framed in an oval medallion on *cdv*, cabinet and postcard mounts. This style of presentation occurred broadly 1860s–early 1900s, but format and fashion clues can help with closer dating.

**34. Cabinet card, *c.* 1905–10.** Edwardian portraits often show subjects in a three-quarter or full-length composition. 'Outdoor' settings typically used painted backcloths suggesting a wooded landscape, while masonry in the foreground included plinths, pedestals and balustrades.

Meanwhile, another type of head and shoulders or short half-length portrait sometimes found in picture collections is the photograph framed in an oval medallion (Figs 33 and 51). This general style of presentation was used periodically between the 1860s and early 1900s, so as a composition it does not offer any firm dating clues. Typically, close-up head and shoulders or short half-length portraits offer no background detail, so hairstyles and upper dress details provide the best dating clues for these photographs.

Early twentieth-century studio photographs usually portray their subjects posing in full-length or three-quarter-length mode, in a variety of settings. During the Edwardian era typical 'outdoor' scenes included a hazy tree-framed glade or woodland background (Figs 34 and 102). There was also a distinct vogue for masonry, so subjects often posed by a 'stone' wall, plinths, pedestals and balustrades (Figs 6 and 34). With indoor scenes sometimes painted scenery conveyed the effect of a traditional drawing room and a curtained window may be sketchily depicted, although often interiors were rather vague (Figs 75, 77 and 78). Various furniture styles were used, although wicker, cane and logs were all natural materials that featured prominently during both the 1890s and early 1900s (Figs 45, 46, 74 and 102).

As explained in Chapter 1, by the 1910s the postcard photograph was more popular than the *carte* or cabinet print, but visual images largely followed familiar conventions. Before and during the First World War, sets and furniture were diverse, reflecting shifting tastes in interior design as the flowing art nouveau aesthetic began to give way to the more modern, angular art deco style. Painted indoor or 'outdoor' sets can still look rather decorative in the early 1910s (Figs 47 and 55), but the growing fashion was for less fussy surroundings: especially common was the blank-walled or wood-panelled room with painted lead-paned windows (Fig. 35). We also notice the introduction of very plain, solid-looking chairs, bench seats and stools from about 1910 onwards (Figs 35 and 47). Interestingly, more live dogs are included in photographs at around this time – animals that must surely have been the subject's own pet, not kept by the studio (Fig. 35).

During the inter-war era, as amateur photography became more widespread, we notice in our collections a gradual shift away from commercial portraits towards casual snapshots. When formal photographs were taken, compositions varied, but the most prominent trend of professional photography between the later 1910s and 1940s was for intimate and clear close-up head and shoulders shots. With close attention paid to camera angle and lighting, a sense of glamour was evoked in these superior portraits that were increasingly reserved for the most special occasions (Figs 36 and 131).

**35. Postcard, c. 1911–14.** Studio room settings of the 1910s often display panelled walls, expanses of faux lead-paned windows and the plainer furniture that was then coming into vogue. Dogs also feature in photographs more often by this time.

**36. Studio portrait, 1930s.**
Between the wars, intimate head and shoulders portraits were very popular and, with close attention to lighting and camera angle, they achieved a new sense of glamour.

## Outdoor Scenes

Unlike formal studio portraits posed in a contrived setting, photographs taken away from the studio represent family members in their own natural environments. Throughout the period covered by this book, the vast majority of non-studio photographs were set outside in the open air, where there was plenty of natural light: indoor domestic photography was uncommon until the development of modern flashbulbs made it easier and safer to illuminate room interiors. Most photograph collections include a significant number of outdoor scenes, whether professional images or amateur snapshots.

## Professional Outdoor Photographs

Some of our old family photographs set outdoors may well have been taken by commercial photographers. These scenes are often set in the garden of the family home and usually demonstrate careful composition of their subjects and a professional picture quality. Chairs and tables and even potted plants and other ornaments were sometimes brought outdoors and arranged to create

**37. Cabinet card,** *c.* **1904–9.** Victorian and Edwardian outdoor photographs were often taken by professional photographers. The lack of studio details on this cabinet mount suggests that this scene set in a domestic garden was taken by an itinerant photographer.

a more picturesque setting, even if the location was the side passage or back yard of a modest terraced house (Fig. 37).

It was not unusual for clients to hire a representative from a local photography studio to attend them at home: photographic evidence suggests that this was especially common when large numbers of people, elderly folk or small children were to be included in the scene, rendering a home visit more convenient.

Alternatively, surviving professional outdoor photographs may be the work of itinerant photographers. From the earliest days of commercial photography, some operators travelled around with their equipment and were welcomed in remoter districts where there was no resident photographer. Their varied clientele included the local gentry and clergy, school teachers, farmers, domestic servants, tradesmen and labourers: sometimes customers would visit the photographer's mobile studio, or they arranged for him to come to their home. The rural trade gradually declined as railway networks and road systems improved and suburban districts developed, but many itinerants continued in business by offering on the spot 'pavement portraits' of customers on the street outside their house, on their doorsteps or in front of their shops or other places of work. Photographs taken by itinerant photographers may theoretically date from as early as the 1850s or 1860s, although most surviving examples in family collections originated in the later nineteenth or early twentieth centuries.

Some outdoor or travelling photographers, or representatives from local studios set up at popular locations that were certain to attract passing custom, especially on weekends and on bank holidays, for example at race meetings, fairs, the seaside, municipal parks, commons and local beauty spots, as seen in Fig. 4. Souvenir photographs taken in public settings during the Victorian era may include glass ambrotypes, *cdvs*, cabinet prints and tintypes, the humble tintype taking open-air photography well into the twentieth century. Meanwhile, another popular tourist photograph that often occurs in family collections is the 'walking picture' – the spontaneous shot taken on the pier or promenade of a seaside resort, but sometimes on busy city pavements: street photographers working for a local company snapped pedestrians unawares as they strolled by, literally capturing them in mid-step, as seen in Figs 38 and 65. They were given a docket and then, if they wished to view and purchase a photograph, they would visit the kiosk later the same day or on the next. These photographs – often holiday souvenirs – enjoyed a long period of popularity in Britain: surviving examples may date from anywhere between about 1920 and the early 1970s, although their heyday was the 1930s and 1940s: these photographs were often printed on postcards.

**38. Walking picture (postcard), early 1930s.** A type of professional outdoor photograph commonly found in family collections is the 'walking picture', which usually dates broadly from between the 1920s and 1960s.

## Open-air Snapshots

The most common kind of outdoor photograph to occur in family collections is the amateur snapshot, taken using a personal camera. As explained in Chapter 1, a few families may discover photographs taken by Victorian or Edwardian ancestors who were keen amateur photographers: see, for example, Figs 68 and 97. However, few households owned their own camera until at least the 1910s and so most of our surviving family snapshots are more modern scenes dating from within the last century (Figs 7, 39, 48–9 and many other examples throughout the book). Usually, amateur snapshots can be distinguished fairly easily from the professional outdoor photograph from their more casual, relaxed poses and, typically, from their imperfect picture composition and image quality: frequently subjects are squinting into the sun and may appear over-exposed; they can be poorly centred in the picture and feet may be cut off. It isn't essential to know whether a photograph was taken by an amateur or professional photographer, but recognising one from the other can help in a general way with dating, for most amateur snapshots originated during the twentieth century, while professional outdoor photographs may well be of earlier date.

**39. Amateur snapshot, *c.* 1936.** The amateur 'snapshots' surviving in today's collections most often date from the 1910s onwards, when more families took up photography. Visual clues such as dress details and any vehicles in the scene can often aid close dating.

## Dating Outdoor Photographs
### Formats
The preceding sections have covered the various types of outdoor photograph that may occur in family collections. As explained in Chapter 1, certain photographic formats were fashionable at specific times and their dates of production also apply to professional outdoor photographs. Of the Victorian formats, ambrotypes and tintypes were most commonly taken outdoors, while early twentieth-century professional outdoor photographs are often tintypes or postcards. Otherwise, our open-air photographic scenes are chiefly amateur snapshots, most common from the 1910s onwards.

### Photographer Information and Mount Styles
Sometimes outdoor *carte*, cabinet or postcard photographs are printed with the details of a professional studio and investigating the photographer's operational dates in the ways outlined in Chapter 2 can help with closer dating (Fig. 4). However, when a professional outdoor photograph is mounted onto a blank *cdv* or cabinet mount, as seen in Fig. 37, this strongly suggests that the photographer was an itinerant operator with no fixed premises. In such cases, perhaps the shape, thickness, colour and any decorative motifs on the mount can be roughly dated, following the guidelines set out in Chapter 3. Naturally, amateur snapshots bear no official photographer details either, but sometimes they have been annotated with the date and names of the subjects, perhaps even the location: such inscriptions were often written by the family photographer or someone appearing in the photograph, so the information is likely to be accurate.

### Visual Evidence
Ultimately, many of our outdoor photographs are undated and unidentified, yet it is important to establish an accurate circa date, in order to understand their context and meaning and to work out possible identities and locations where the faces and places are unknown. In many cases all we have to go on is the visual image itself and it can be hard to know where to start, but it helps to remember that essentially outdoor photographs provide an authentic view of the past: not only the people pictured in these scenes, but also the natural landscapes or built urban spaces, the solid structures and moveable vehicles all existed at one time, even if they have changed significantly over time or have not survived into the present century. Every street, shop, public house, church, dwelling, farm or beach, model of car, style of bicycle and so on pictured in a family photograph has a history or timeline that can potentially be researched, using a variety of sources.

Admittedly, we may never be able firmly to identify and locate an anonymous field or landscape, as seen, for example, in Fig. 54: in these instances the only visual clues are the clothes worn by the subjects, so dating rests on identifying and pinpointing the fashions. However, many outdoor scenes contain other pictorial clues, especially buildings, streetscapes and vehicles. The design of a building may be relevant when dating an image if its architectural style is recognisable, such as the twentieth-century properties seen in Figs 88 and 100, which offer firm 1930s and 1950s *post quem* dates for those images respectively; however, older structures are of less help since family members may have been pictured outside a historic property built centuries earlier. Photographs of ancestors and relatives photographed at home are a common genre of outdoor photography and are examined in more detail in Chapter 11.

Assigning an approximate date to scenes that include streetscapes and public buildings can be successful, especially if any local names are displayed, such as street signs or the names of shops, a church, pub, village hall, garage or place of work. The Internet is a powerful tool when dating and investigating elements of outdoor photographs: for example, carrying out a simple Google search for the name of a shop pictured in a photograph may reveal trade-directory or census information, even other dated photographs of the building with which to compare the family snapshot. Historypin is also a great image-sharing website formed like a map that allows users to search for old images by location and date, compare photographs of different time periods and to add their own vintage photographs: www.historypin.com. In fact, family photographs often have firm connections to the geographical area in which they were taken and we explore this subject more fully in Chapter 13.

Many outdoor photographs depict vehicles of various descriptions, whether horse-drawn carriages, carts or farm vehicles (Figs 105 and 148), buses, charabancs (Fig. 107), vans, cars (Figs 39, 108 and 144), motorbikes (Fig. 64), bicycles (Fig. 106) or even prams (Fig. 103). When vehicles occur in photographs, their style and any other relevant features can often aid accurate dating. Broadly, no motor-powered vehicles are likely to occur in Victorian photographs but horse-drawn conveyances may conceivably occur throughout the entire period covered by this book. Public street transport became motorised during the early twentieth century, although both horse-drawn and electric trams and horse-drawn and motorised buses and charabancs co-existed in the early 1900s. Motorised commercial vehicles also became increasingly common during the early–mid twentieth century, although some tradesmen were still using traditional horse-drawn carts and wagons in the 1940s and beyond. Similarly, farm equipment might be mechanical or horse-drawn during the early twentieth century. Relatively few ordinary families owned a motor car until after the Second World War, although private car ownership gradually rose from the early 1900s onwards, especially during the 1920s, and our more affluent ancestors may have been early motorists.

No single source of information exists to help with dating the wide variety of vehicles that may occur in family photographs, but a number of organisations and independent enthusiasts and collectors run specialist websites. Perhaps the most important resource for discovering more about motor vehicles is the website of the Surrey Vintage Vehicle Society (SVVS): www.svvs.org. This displays thousands of twentieth-century vehicle-related images, which provide useful comparisons for family photographs, while inquiries can be submitted via its 'Help' page. SVVS experts may be able to identify and date commercial, agricultural and domestic vehicles in old photographs, often advising on their make, model and manufacture; additionally, where the registration plate is visible, they will perhaps be able to confirm the year and county of its registration. Meanwhile, another useful website for researching historic cars is Old Classic Car: www.oldclassiccar. co.uk – which includes a Car Registration Numbers Index. There is considerable interest today in vintage and classic cars and some major car manufacturers have a heritage division within their organisation, even an archivist who looks after historical material and who may be able to advise on relevant vehicles pictured in family photographs. Bearing in mind that the year of a car's registration does not necessarily indicate the precise year of a photograph, it does nonetheless provide a useful *post quem* date, and this may turn out to be one of the most valuable picture-dating clues.

*Chapter 5*

# DATING THE VISUAL IMAGE: FASHION CLUES

There is no escaping the reality that in some family photographs there is little to see or to go on, except the human subject(s) of the picture: even when there are other pictorial elements that can be researched, generally it is the appearance of our ancestors and relatives – both their physical characteristics and their attire – that particularly captures our attention. The fashions worn in the past may appear very different to today's modes and immediately confirm that we are viewing an image from another era. Dating clothing, hairstyles and accessories is not the easiest process for the average researcher, but it is an accurate method and in some cases assessing the fashions may be the *only* way of estimating when a photograph was taken.

A question frequently raised by family historians when examining the dress in old photographs is whether their poorer ancestors would have been able to follow fashion closely – that is, whether they may have looked up to date, despite their humble status, or whether they are likely to have been wearing very outmoded clothes. This is a significant point and suggests that before we look at how to recognise historical dress styles, we should consider how fashion may have impacted on past generations.

## Following Fashion

By the time portrait photography reached a mass market in the 1860s, fashion information was becoming more accessible via fashion plates and paper sewing patterns in women's magazines, while widely circulated *carte de visite* photographs of royalty, aristocracy, actresses and other 'celebrities' provided popular images of the fashion leaders of the day. By the late 1800s many newspapers published illustrated advertisements for consumer goods and mail-order catalogues illustrated their wares: as the literacy of the general public improved, people could view and read about the latest fashions in print. Anyone could visit a sizeable town or city to see at first hand what was being worn in the streets by the prosperous classes, or to view goods in the windows of drapery shops, outfitters and department stores. Professional tailors, dressmakers and milliners also kept abreast of new trends and many stocked fashionable materials and trimmings for their customers.

Gentlemen typically visited their favourite tailor for bespoke coats and suits, although decent, affordable 'off-the-peg' lounge or business suits were already available for ordinary working men. By contrast, relatively few female garments could be purchased ready-made in the Victorian era, since ladies' fashions were generally more complex and required a skilled hand for accurate styling and intricate ornamentation. A wide selection of ready-to-wear female fashions only became available between the wars when simpler clothing styles aided mass-production and inexpensive chain stores proliferated throughout Britain. Traditionally, most of our female ancestors learnt to sew when young and many women assembled undergarments, shirts and other small articles at home, some making dresses and outerwear too: indeed, many sewed, altered and mended garments for a living. However, if family members were not very competent needlewomen or had no time for home dressmaking, numerous professional tailors, dressmakers and seamstresses catered for all sectors of the market, including an ordinary lower middle or working class clientele.

Fashion news and clothing options were plentiful throughout much of the period covered by this book, with many tradesmen operating in rural areas, as well as urban centres. When our working forebears bought, made or ordered new clothes and accessories they could, if they wished, follow the most up-to-date modes – or a version of fashionable dress, to suit their personal taste: certainly many went to great efforts with the 'best' outfit that would be kept for church on Sundays and other special occasions. The most expensive part of a new ensemble was the material and an enormous variety of textiles were available by the mid-nineteenth century to suit all pockets and seasons of the year, from fine silks to plain woollen cloth, workaday cottons, linens and mixed fabrics. The quality of the material and extravagance of trimmings distinguished the dress of the wealthy from that of the working classes – not the basic cut or shape of their clothes. When the style of garments grew outmoded, if still wearable they were often re-modelled to reflect changing fashions: surplus fabric was kept from the original making of the garment for the purpose of alterations and repairs. Unfortunately, our most impoverished ancestors with little or no income only rarely acquired new clothes, instead relying on a combination of charity, cast-offs, clothing clubs, second-hand garments from dealers or low-quality goods from market stalls.

## Dress in Photographs

Accurate historical information about the poorer sectors of society tends to be elusive, but photographic evidence (or lack of) suggests that ancestors who struggled to earn a basic living or were genuinely impoverished never sat for a professional photographic portrait, unless it was a workhouse photograph or, worse, a criminal 'mug-shot': certainly, this would explain why we never see figures wearing ragged clothing in regular family photographs. However, the occupational data surrounding identified images confirms that many ancestors and relatives from the lower working classes visited their local photographer on occasion and invariably presented a respectable, even stylish appearance that may seem to belie their social status as seamstresses, domestic servants, miners, fishermen, farm hands and so on. Judging from certain images, we might even speculate whether the desire to display a flattering outfit or new hairstyle may sometimes have been instrumental in prompting a visit to the local photographer (see Figs 43(a) and (b)). Victorian and Edwardian women's fashions were particularly distinctive and there seems to be a correlation between photography and the opportunity for personal display: it is no coincidence that in the mid–late nineteenth century on average two adult females to every male were photographed in the studio.

**40. Cabinet card, late 1890s.** Usually our ancestors wore their best, most fashionable clothes for a formal photograph, although some studios kept theatrical dress or other picturesque clothing for clients to dress up in. Highland dress was popular with tourists to Scotland.

It was generally understood that clients would arrive at the studio wearing their finest, most fashionable clothing: prosperous ancestors generally had several elegant ensembles from which to choose, while those of lesser means donned their 'Sunday best' suit or gown and accessories. Whatever their social background, clearly our forebears wished to present themselves in the best possible light, to create a good impression in the special portraits that would be circulated among family and friends and perhaps eventually displayed in an album. The general practice of wearing one's best outfit answers another query that often arises: some researchers have formed the idea that the clothing seen in studio photographs did not belong to its wearers but was 'lent' by the photographer. However, there is no firm historical evidence to support this notion: as discussed, ordinary working people usually possessed at least one good outfit, and bearing in mind that many ancestors (especially females) had their garments individually made to achieve the correct fit necessary for comfort and appearance, we realise that local photographers could not possibly have kept a stock of fashionable male, female, adult and juvenile clothing to fit every prospective client, whatever their height and build.

Occasionally, our ancestors did 'dress up' for a photograph in special items kept by the studio, but generally this was 'fancy dress' of a theatrical or picturesque nature – perhaps an exotic Japanese kimono, or, for example, a romantic Highland outfit, popular with tourists visiting Scotland (Fig. 40): such fanciful attire bears little or no resemblance to regular dress. Now and again a photograph may display regional dress, for example, genuine nineteenth-century photographs of female Welsh ancestors wearing their traditional national costume. Some photographs depict forebears wearing military uniforms or distinctive occupational attire – themes that are examined in Part Three.

## Dating Fashion in Photographs

Nineteenth- and twentieth-century fashions in clothing, hairstyles, headwear, footwear, jewellery and other accessories have been expertly researched and their periods of use established by dress historians, enabling identification and successful dating of the dress details displayed in old photographs. Essentially, it was the shape, or silhouette, of clothing on the body which defined the style of a given era. The fashionable female silhouette was formed by the corsets, crinolines, bustles and other foundation garments worn beneath clothing, which produced a succession of very distinctive, dateable 'looks', the over all effect of an outfit being completed by complementary sleeve shapes, coiffures, headwear, personal ornaments and dress trimmings. Because female fashions altered regularly in the past, adult women's dress can often be dated accurately to within around five or six years, sometimes less. Conversely, men's garments were more standardised and uniform, the main developments effected by subtle shifts in tailoring that produced either a slender or bulkier silhouette. Styles of neck wear, hairstyles, facial hair and hats did alter over time, but might be influenced as much by personal taste or by the occasion, as by fashion, and can therefore be harder to pinpoint precisely. Because of this, typically the appearance of male ancestors in photographs is dateable to within around ten to fifteen years.

Children wore garments that followed juvenile conventions but also echoed adult styles, their clothing acquiring a more 'grown-up' appearance as they became older, as seen, for example, in Fig. 60. Boys often dressed as men in suits with long trousers by the age of around 11 in the Victorian era and in later periods in their early 'teens' (a word not used until the twentieth century), the adoption of adult men's wear often coinciding with their entry into full-time work. Girls steadily lowered the hems of their skirts as they advanced through childhood and adolescence, finally adopting full-length hemlines, firmly fitted corsets and putting their long hair up, like women, when aged between around 15 and 17 years (see the Coming of Age section in Chapter 6).

Predictably, young adults aged in their late 'teens' and twenties usually appear the most fashionably dressed in photographs and so their images typically provide the most accurate dating clues: like the youth of all generations, many of our young ancestors and relatives were naturally interested in new trends and, if employed, while single often had more disposable income to spend on personal items than later, once there were children to support. Many mature family members also maintained a keen sense of style and would dress with great care for a formal photograph, in accordance with what was deemed suitable for their age and status (Fig. 78). Middle-aged and, especially, elderly ancestors and relatives are usually attired the most conservatively in photographs: many older ladies wore sedate black garments, were slower to adopt new styles and sometimes modified the more extreme fashion features of the day to suit their expanding figures and advancing years. That said, recognisable elements of older ladies' dress are dateable in their own right, for example matronly day caps (Figs 31, 81, 82 and 86) and demure bonnets (Figs 45 and 79). In general, in mixed group photographs such as wedding scenes or large family gatherings, it is the appearance of young adults and, especially, that of younger women that offers the closest date range for the entire scene. With photographs portraying only older subjects, we may need to consider a wider date range for the image.

Many family historians are interested in historical fashions and may have already estimated the general period of some of their photographs, but few are confident enough to date dress details with certainty. For readers with a rudimentary knowledge of past fashions there are various recommended publications by dress historians to help with identifying and dating fashion features in photographs: the most useful guides are listed in the Sources section. It can also be very helpful to search online, using Google Images, for example, to search for dated fashion plates or to view *firmly dated* photographs, with which to compare family photographs. A detailed visual survey of fashion is not possible here, but below is a summary of the main dress developments that researchers are likely to encounter in their own photographs. Each feature mentioned is exemplified in the photographs reproduced in this chapter and throughout the book.

## Dating Women's Dress, 1840s–1940s
### 1840s–68
During the earliest decades of photography the fashionable silhouette comprised a fitted bodice and a full, bell-shaped skirt, which grew even wider following the introduction of the crinoline in 1856, a circular cage-like frame worn beneath the clothes. By the later 1840s narrow sleeves were giving way to the flared *pagoda* style: this shape dominated the 1850s (Fig. 2) and continued into the early 1860s, although closed sleeves fitted at the cuff may occur towards the end of the 1850s and were established as the prevailing fashion by 1862/3. At this time skirts were vast in circumference, as we see in full-length *carte de visite* photographs of early–mid decade (Figs 3 and 86) and in outdoor scenes of the era (Fig. 97). From around mid-decade onwards, fashionable gowns progressively shed their bulk, the front of the skirt steadily growing flatter, the back becoming more pronounced and the material behind extending into a sweeping train (Fig. 41). Sometimes stylish outdoor garments were worn to the studio: cloaks and shawls were popular during the 1850s and were still worn by older ladies in the 1860s (Fig. 86), while more fashionable short, wide jackets were favoured by young women (Fig. 41).

The principal hairstyle of the early–mid 1840s was curled ringlets, and some older ladies retained this style into the 1860s, although hair may be partly concealed when older or mature married ladies wore a day cap, as was customary in the mid-1800s (Figs 81, 82 and 86). More usually, and in the case of younger women, throughout the later 1840s, 1850s and turn of the 1860s hair was centrally parted and often dressed smoothly over the ears into a low chignon behind (Figs 2 and 86). During the early 1860s, the hair began to be drawn back behind the ears (Figs 3 and 41) and from mid-decade onwards the chignon was worn increasingly high behind the head (Fig. 89). Bonnets were usual for outdoors until the early 1860s and continued to be favoured by the older generation, although younger women often chose neat, round 'pork pie' hats edged with feathers or fur (Figs 3 and 41) or decorative straw hats.

**41.** *Carte de visite, c.* **1865–7.** From the mid-1860s onwards the wide crinoline skirt grew flatter in front, the back material often extending into a sweeping train. This lady also wears a short, wide jacket and carries a neat 'pork pie' hat, both fashionable for much of the decade.

**42. *Carte de visite, c.* 1872.** This prosperous ancestor wears a luxurious version of early 1870s fashions, her silk, lace-trimmed gown clearly displaying the protruding bustle and back drapery, in vogue *c.* 1869/70–5. Her tall hairstyle incorporating a plait is typical of the 1870s.

## 1869–75

A new silhouette becomes evident in photographs by around 1869 or 1870, gowns having altered shape during the mid–late 1860s: by the turn of the decade the increasing bulk of back skirt material was being raised up over a *tournure* or bustle – a projecting pad worn behind the waist beneath the clothes. The new style required layered garments, photographs of the early 1870s displaying overdresses draped up in swathes, to accommodate the new silhouette (Figs 4, 28 and 42). The exuberant, feminine look remained in vogue until mid-decade, fashionable bodices featuring a choice of open or closed sleeves and either high necklines complemented by a frill, a bow or jabot (Fig. 4), or a V or square-shaped neckline ornamented with lace and set off by a velvet ribbon choker at the throat (Figs 28 and 42). Hairstyles were also especially elaborate at this time, the chignon typically worn high on the head and sometimes incorporating plaits and/or coils of long hair, as seen in the above examples.

## 1876–83

In around the mid-1870s, photographs reveal another stylistic shift, precipitated by a new under structure, the long, rigid cuirass corset that extended in a continuous line over the hips, forcing the early 1870s bustle downwards. A narrower silhouette evolved during the later 1870s as skirts were drawn or gathered closely across the legs at the front (Fig. 43(a)), while residual back drapery now cascaded downwards at the back of the skirt. The tightening lines of fashion inspired different garments and the new outfit generally comprised either a hip-length fitted bodice and skirt or a slender, front-buttoning one-piece 'princess' dress, both styles featuring narrow sleeves. Until *c.* 1880 the skirt ended in a train (Fig. 43(a)), but afterwards trains grew outmoded for daywear and were retained mainly for evening dress. In the later 1870s some young women and fashionable older ladies began to wear their hair curled or softly waved with a short fringe, a distinctive style that also occurs in photographs of the 1880s.

During the early 1880s the silhouette was characteristically very narrow and sheath-like: fashionable skirts were often worn well off the ground and were typically ornamented with gathers, ruches, shirring and rows of pleats (Figs 31 and 43(b)). Close-fitting bodices fastened down the front with tiny buttons; rather plain in style, they were often accessorised with a round white or dark lace collar and/or heavy gold jewellery such as a large pendant or locket suspended on a short chain (Figs 43(b) and 76). Throughout the later 1870s and 1880s there was a great fondness for sumptuous silk velvet and 'plush' (cotton velvet) materials: garments might be fashioned entirely from velvet or plush (Figs 31 and 76), or bodices and skirts might display contrasting fabrics, dark

**43. *Carte de visite*: (a) *c.* 1878–80; (b) *c.* 1880–2.**
These two photos of the same person were taken perhaps only a year or so apart. Her bodice showing the late 1870s/early 1880s cuirass line is identical in each, but she updated her hair and accessories and wore a new, untrained skirt for the second photo.

**44. *Carte de visite, c.. 1886–9.*
Here four daughters, including at least two domestic servants, pose with their father, a coastguard. The girls all wear fashionable mid–late 1880s daywear: note the pleated skirts, deep bustle projection and tight-fitting bodices with contrasting velvet panels.

woollen cloth often juxtaposed with velvet or silk trimmings and panels (Figs 31 and 43).

## 1884–9

In around 1883 high fashion decreed a return of the bustle and by 1884 signs of the new style may occur in family photographs. Between 1885 and 1888/9, the bustle projection was a prominent feature and could be very pronounced, jutting out sharply behind the waist, the front of the skirt usually layered and the upper fabric draped apron-style over a pleated or plain under skirt (Fig. 44). By c. 1889 the bustle was diminishing, although there was residual padding around the hips (Fig. 90). During the mid–late 1880s, the close-fitting bodice developed even narrower sleeves and a high, tight neckline, creating a severe effect, although bodice styling became more complex: the popular *plastron* front featured contrasting fabric inserts, a mock waistcoat-style front also fashionable (Figs 44 and 90). Many girls and some young women still favoured a short fringe, although a sleeker hairstyle was developing by the late 1880s, the front hair drawn up and dressed into a high chignon (Fig. 44). Meanwhile, headwear changed again: the neat, round hats and brimless *tocques* of the early 1880s gave way by to taller headwear, a narrow, towering hat or bonnet in vogue between c. 1886 and 1890 (Fig. 90).

## 1890s

By 1890 the bustle was outmoded but photographs still demonstrate some residual shaping around the hips and a slight draped front to the skirt, a tight-fitting, high-collared, panelled bodice continuing late-1880s modes (Fig. 74). What becomes most significant now is the shape of ladies' sleeves and these provide the most useful fashion dating feature of the decade. Between about 1890 and 1892 usually a small vertical puff is noticed at the shoulder – a sign that the *gigot* or 'leg-o'-mutton' sleeve was forming (Figs 74 and 87 – different portrayals of the same ancestor). During 1893 and 1894 photographs demonstrate the increasing fullness of sleeves in the upper arm as the puff expanded (Fig. 71); in 1895 and 1896 sleeves attained their greatest width, displaying a vast, balloon-like shape, especially when worn to extremes by young women (Figs 32, 45 and 91). This exaggerated sleeve style was also matched by elaborate bodices for formal wear, contrasting panels, bows, lace inserts and collars and other decorative details accentuating the ornate effect. Even hairstyles grew fuller around mid-decade as fashionable women began to wear softer styles, the front hair slightly frizzed, waved or rolled back off the face (Fig. 32). These coiffures were balanced by wide-brimmed hats that rested plate-like on the head, ornamented with bows, flowers and feathers (Figs 45 and 91). By the later 1890s the sleeve puff was beginning to deflate and to

**45. *Carte de visite, c.* 1895–6.** Puffed 'leg-o'-mutton' sleeves identify fashions of the 1890s, reaching their greatest width in 1895 and 1896. Formal bodices were very elaborate and young women wore ornate wide-brimmed hats, while older ladies preferred conservative bonnets.

withdraw higher up the arm; finally, between around 1898 and 1900 a narrower sleeve shape was fashionable, with residual detailing at the top of the arm – usually a small puff, a frill or epaulette (Fig. 80).

## 1900–10

During the late 1890s and early 1900s an hourglass silhouette was fashionable, reflecting prevailing art nouveau aesthetic lines. The vogue for a full bosom, small waist and curvaceous hips was demonstrated strikingly in lavish evening wear – rarely seen in family photographs, although a modest version is evident in early twentieth-century day wear (Figs 46 and 102). Formal dress bodices and blouses were puffed in front to emphasise the bust and were embellished

**46. Cabinet card, c. 1901–5.** An hourglass figure was fashionable in the early 1900s: blouses and bodices were puffed in front to accentuate the bust and tailored skirts with a narrow waist fitted the hips smoothly before flaring outwards. These sleeves display the shape of c. 1901–5.

with ornamental frills, lace bands, inserts or collars and rows of narrow vertical tucks, while plain skirts were expertly tailored with shaped panels to display a narrow waist, smooth hip area and a graceful flared hemline (Figs 46, 77 and 102). Blouses and bodices generally featured a high, choker-like neckline for most of the Edwardian era, often complemented by a brooch at the neck. Sleeve shapes again aid closer dating: in 1900 sleeves were generally straight and narrow (Fig. 77); then between 1901 and c. 1904/5 slim-fitting sleeves generally became fuller in the lower arm, before gathering into a cuff at the wrist (Figs 46 and 98); finally, during the period c. 1905–9, focus shifted to the elbow, as expressed in deeper sleeve cuffs, three-quarter length sleeves, or puffs or flounces around elbow level (Figs 34, 92 and 102). Separate blouses, skirts and jackets were also increasingly fashionable: the smart 'tailor-made' suit was becoming an essential outfit, some young women emulating the masculine suit by teaming a plain blouse with a long knotted tie (Fig. 6).

By the early 1900s hairstyles were becoming softer and fuller, the hair sometimes waved and drawn up loosely above the forehead (Figs 46, 77 and 141). Fashionable headwear included summer boaters or wide-brimmed straw hats, the most ornate styles heaped with bows, feathers and flowers (Figs 6, 34, 92 and 98). Like sleeves, the shape of hats can help with more precise dating of Edwardian photographs: in the early 1900s brims were generally wide and crowns were shallow (Figs 46, 85 (centre) and 98); after about 1905/6, the crowns grew larger, creating a vast, gateau-like effect, as seen in Figs 6 and 92.

## 1911–18

During the early 1910s fashion favoured a more natural body shape and a decline in fussy ornamentation – an altogether less cluttered line. Ancestors can look fairly plain in photographs of this period, when wearing the popular blouse and skirt combination that formed the basis of the female wardrobe (Figs 8, 35 and 47). Typically, a white or coloured blouse with a high collar, or slightly lower neckline with a rounded collar, was teamed with a plain tailored skirt, the skirt rather narrow or moderate in shape and sometimes featuring ornamental buttons. The masculine shirt and tie also remained popular just before the First World War, as a business-like working style for young women (Fig. 35) and tailored jackets grew longer, while for formal occasions, narrow one-piece dresses were fashionable. The most fashionable hairstyle of the period 1909–14 was a centre parting, the length of the hair raised into two swathes above the temples (Figs 35, 47 and 122(b)).

In 1915 fashion decreed that the narrow, so-called 'hobble skirt' be abandoned, that hemlines be worn shorter, to mid-calf level, and that skirts and dresses become wider at the hem. In practice, many ordinary women wore skirts of moderate width throughout the decade, although sometimes the shift

**47. Postcard, *c*. 1910–13.** A white or coloured blouse and plain tailored skirt were usual for daywear during the 1910s, skirts often rather narrow early in the decade and featuring ornamental buttons. These young women's fashionable hairstyles are typical of *c*. 1910–13.

to a shorter, flared skirt is evident in photographs and with the lower leg on display from the mid-1910s onwards, shoes came into vogue (Fig. 93). Other major changes were the decline of the high choker neckline and preference for lower rounded or V-shaped dress or blouse necklines with a collar attached, the collars becoming larger after mid-decade (Figs 93, 104, 118 and 127–8). For outdoors, loosely belted jackets and wide-brimmed hats that skimmed the head were fashionable during the later 1910s (Figs 104, 123 and 127–8). Naturally, many photographs of this period include military and other wartime uniforms: these are discussed in Chapter 12.

**48. Amateur snapshot, dated 1920.** Between about 1918 and 1922, frocks and suits were rather loose and 'barrel-shaped' and hemlines were set at mid–low calf length. Broadbrimmed hats with deep crowns were often worn by young women, although various styles were fashionable.

## 1919–30

Post-First World War photographs demonstrate how garments remained relatively loose: sometimes dresses of *c.* 1918 through to *c.* 1922 display a barrel-like silhouette, the waistline perhaps a little higher than natural level and the skirt fabric billowing towards a straight, low calf-length hemline (Figs 7 and 48). Prominent collars lie flat over the shoulders or are formed as reveres. Some young women had cut their hair short during the later war years, or did so soon afterwards: therefore, bobbed hair is seen increasingly in photographs, becoming common during the early 1920s, while a more conservative alternative was for longer hair to be neatly pinned back (Fig. 7). Headwear was very varied in the early–mid 1920s: wide-brimmed and narrower helmet-like hats usually displayed deep crowns, while squashy berets were fashionable with the young (Figs 48, 94 and 107).

Stylistic shifts are evident in photographs from around 1923 onwards. Straight, untailored dresses were left unbelted or secured loosely with a fabric belt at dropped waist level. Collars persisted, although the most fashionable necklines were either V-shaped or rounded, the plainer neck area sometimes set off by a string of pearls or beads. Hemlines offer important dating clues for the 1920s: where figures are posed in full-length we see how garments remained relatively long until at least 1925, generally set at mid–low calf level (Figs 7 and 48), but between around 1926 and 1930, hemlines rose dramatically. Young women of the so-called 'flapper' era wore the shortest dresses and skirts, ending on or just below the knee, this fashion extending to smart suits, bridal wear, narrow coats and simple shift-like dresses for summer, worn with pale or flesh-coloured stockings and bar shoes (Fig. 56). Short cropped hair is also seen more often in photographs, many older ladies adopting a bob during the late 1920s; by this time, the close-fitting cloche hat, pulled down low over the forehead, was the most popular style (Figs 56 and 151). Fur collars, stoles and wraps were also major fashion statements, especially fox furs, worn by women from all walks of life.

## 1930s

Although this decade is within living memory for some, the appearance of relatives in 1930s images can be difficult to date accurately. As in the 1920s, hairstyles, hats (when worn) and hemlines provide the most useful dating clues. Full-length photographs show that by around 1930 hemlines were becoming slightly fuller and longer and from 1931/2 until at least 1936, there was a return to calf-length garments fashioned from flowing, draped fabrics, plain or floral-printed for day wear (Figs 38 and 49). In the early–mid 1930s fashionable hairstyles remained short, but often appear softer or are set in

**49. Amateur snapshot, mid-1930s.** Softly draped printed fabrics and calf-length hemlines help to date photographs of the early–mid 1930s. Short hair set in pronounced waves was also fashionable at this time.

pronounced waves (Figs 36, 39, 49 and 95). Hats of this period include the close-fitting late-1920s cloche, soft berets and pull-on beanie styles, or wide-brimmed picture hats for summer. From around 1936/7 onwards, a changing silhouette becomes evident – a sharper, more tailored look that was well-established by the outbreak of war in 1939. Late-decade photographs reveal squarer padded shoulders, perhaps short puffed sleeves, smart fitted dresses, lapelled jackets and shorter hemlines again (Figs 112 and 113). Hats of the later 1930s were also more structured, often asymmetrical or worn at an angle, while hair was sometimes grown longer, to around collar length. Many family photographs from the 1930s are relaxed snapshots and in these we see sleeveless sundresses now being worn in summer (Fig. 39), while beach scenes reveal new designs in swimwear – bathing costumes that were becoming more revealing and streamlined (Fig. 109).

## 1940s

The Second World War and its aftermath dominated dress during this decade and many 1940s photographs feature women in uniform, as discussed in Chapter 12. Civilian garments were rationed between 1941 and 1949 and the Utility clothing scheme of 1942–52 restricted amounts of clothing fabric and trimmings (including buttons), inspiring an economical, yet smart female style. Material shortages dictated that dresses and skirts ended just below the knee and were slightly A-line in shape, either plain or featuring modest pleats (Figs 9, 65 and 100). Dresses, jackets and coats usually had square padded shoulders: bodices were slim-fitting with little or no applied decoration, but were often enlivened by puffed sleeves, draped cowl necklines or ruching (Figs 96, 100 and 108). Under the growing influence of American fashion, casual separates became increasingly popular, jerseys and skirts a common choice with the younger generation (Fig. 100 – right), even slacks. Everyday footwear usually comprised a sensible leather laced shoe with a small heel (Figs 9, 65 and 100), or for summer substantial sandals, although more stylish court shoes were a smarter alternative. Hair, growing longer since the late 1930s, was curled, waved or rolled off the face during the 1940s, presenting a feminine, glamorous image (Figs 9, 96, 100 and 108).

## Dating Men's Dress, 1840s–1940s
### 1840s and 1850s

In photographs of the 1840s and 1850s, we see the slender silhouette typical of the early Victorian era. A slim-fitting frock coat was worn with narrow trousers and, usually, a deep V-fronted waistcoat that exposed the shirt front (Fig. 1); neck wear completed the outfit, a black or coloured silk cravat or horizontal bow tie being common choices (Figs 1 and 26). Until the mid-1850s facial hair usually comprised prominent sideburns, but from then onwards some men began to wear beards.

### 1860s and 1870s

Men's clothing became more diverse during the 1860s. An elegant knee-length frock coat was a formal option, worn with matching or contrasting trousers and the traditional dark cravat or horizontal bow tie (Fig. 50). The morning coat with rounded front edges was a semi-formal alternative, tailored either in dark cloth matching the other suit pieces (Fig. 27), or in velvet material (Fig. 89). A new garment introduced during the 1860s was the relaxed lounging jacket, often worn open or with just the top button fastened: at this stage it was worn with paler trousers and teamed with a formal silk top hat or a semi-casual felt hat (Fig. 29). The top hat was still correct for formal occasions (Fig. 89), while a new hat, the bowler, was just coming into vogue (Fig. 97). Hair was often

**50.** *Carte de visite*, **1865.** This affluent ancestor wears the formal knee-length frock coat that changed little between the 1840s and 1860s, his black silk neck tie a conservative choice. His hair is curled above the ears in typical 1860s fashion and, being young, he is clean-shaven.

grown slightly longish and may appear curled above the ears (Figs 27, 50 and 51). As always, youthful men were generally clean-shaven, although mature men often favoured a beard – either the early style of beard that extended underneath the chin (Fig. 27), a bushy beard and moustache (Fig. 89) or the distinctive 'mutton-chop' whiskers, fashionable during the later 1860s and 1870s (Fig. 51).

By the turn of the 1870s the lounging jacket, waistcoat and trousers were developing into a respectable suit that typically comprised three matching pieces (Fig. 52). This rapidly became the working man's 'Sunday best' suit, worn for church, weddings and any other public occasions. A distinguishing feature of late-1860s/1870s jackets and of formal coats is their wide lapels – a useful photograph dating clue (Figs 4, 51 and 52). Trousers were generally rather loose or moderate in cut, although the growing trend as the 1870s advanced was towards a narrower style (Fig. 4). The most common neckwear of this decade was a turned-down shirt collar worn with a long knotted tie – essentially a broader version of today's regular tie (Fig. 52), although slimmer bow ties (Fig. 4) and formal silk cravats (Fig. 51) may also occur. Substantial

**51.** *Carte de visite,* **late 1860s/early 1870s.** Mature Victorian men always wore more facial hair than youths. Beards and moustaches symbolised masculinity and authority: these bushy 'mutton-chop' whiskers were most fashionable in the later 1860s and 1870s.

**52.** *Carte de visite,* **late 1860s/early 1870s.** The three-piece lounge suit became increasingly popular over time and was the 'Sunday best' outfit for ordinary working men. These wide jacket lapels and long knotted tie are characteristic of the late 1860s and 1870s.

facial hair was usual for mature men throughout the 1870s, including the bushy 'mutton-chop' whiskers, still popular (Figs 4 and 51).

## 1880s and 1890s

Late-1870s fashion had encouraged a more slender male silhouette, echoing developments in female dress, and we notice this continuing throughout the 1880s and 1890s. Lounge jackets and trousers appear narrower in cut, while a remodelled version of the sloping morning coat was highly fashionable by the 1880s (Figs 72 and 90). Typically men's coat or jacket lapels were small and neat during the 1880s and 1890s and may be edged with silk-braid binding, while a white handkerchief in the outer top pocket became firmly established as a fashionable accessory (Figs 53, 72 and 90) and a gold watch chain looped across the waistcoat front was virtually obligatory for the respectable late-

Victorian male (Figs 53, 90 and 91). Neckwear was less prominent at this time as coats and jackets usually fastened high at the neck: some men retained the turned-down collar, although both a high standing starched collar and winged collar were becoming fashionable in the late nineteenth century (Figs 5, 31, 53 and 91).

By the late 1880s and early 1890s, an extremely slender look had evolved for the most fashionable young men, sometimes accentuated by narrow, vertically striped trousers (Fig. 53). Bowler hats were worn with most outfits (except for the conservative frock coat, which required the formal top hat), and acquired tall crowns during the later 1880s and early 1890s – a helpful dating clue (Figs 5, 53, 90 and 142). Generally, bowler crowns had lowered to a moderate height by the mid-1890s (Fig. 91), although some older men retained the tall style in the early 1900s. As before, very young men often went clean-shaven, while men aged in their later twenties and thirties were beginning to discard the beard, often preferring a neat moustache (Figs 90 and 91). To the conservative, however, the beard remained symbolic of Victorian dignity and authority and older men retained beards throughout the 1890s and beyond (Fig. 5).

**53.** *Carte de visite,* **late 1880s/early 1890s.** Men's garments grew neater and narrower during the 1880s and 1890s, with tall bowler hats accentuating the slender style. A stylish morning coat with sloping front edges was often worn with pin-striped trousers for special occasions.

## 1900–10

Men's appearance altered only subtly in the new century and remained fairly static until after the First World War. The regular lounge suit was slim-fitting but sometimes appears slightly easier in cut than during the late-Victoria era. It was usually worn in three matching pieces, and in some photographs presents a crisp, rather stark appearance (Fig. 75). The lounge jacket was typically quite long and the lapels generally short to moderate in the early 1900s (Figs 54, 58, 75, 77 and 92), but becoming longer during the 1910s – one of the few distinctive features that can help with closer dating of early twentieth-century menswear (Figs 55 and 93). When viewed in full length, throughout the early 1900s and 1910s trousers tend to appear rather narrow:

also being short in length, they reveal an expanse of laced boot, which remained the usual footwear until at least the First World War (Figs 55, 75 and 93). High starched 1890s shirt collars drifted over into the early 1900s, both standing and winged collars appearing in early twentieth-century photographs (Figs 58 and 143). Winged collars remained a conservative option, although the main Edwardian trend was for the more modern turned-down shirt collar, teamed with the long knotted tie: at this time the turned-down collar was heavily starched and often featured rounded points (Figs 75, 77, 92 and 93).

Fashions in facial hair continually evolved, expressing the growing preference for a modern, fresher look as the twentieth century unfolded. Most young men went completely clean-shaven during the early 1900s and this was the norm during the 1910s. Mature and middle-aged men might follow suit, although some favoured a moustache until at least the First World War (Figs 54, 58, 77, 78 and 143), a neat, trimmed beard being retained by many elderly men. Headwear included the bowler hat, still worn, for example, for formal business wear by the conservative and also by working men for special

**54. Outdoor scene, *c.* 1900–5.** The three-piece lounge suit was regular daywear for most Edwardian men. Winged, standing or turned-down starched shirt collars were usually teamed with knotted ties. Cloth caps became popular, although bowlers, boaters and homburgs were also worn.

**55. Postcard, 1910s.** Suits were very slim-fitting during the 1910s. Jackets developed longer lapels and narrow trousers were worn to ankle length, revealing laced leather boots. Cloth caps remained popular with working males, growing flatter and wider by this date.

occasions (Fig. 54). However, softer felt hats with a dented crown, like the homburg and fedora, were more stylish options (Fig. 54), while boaters and other straw hats with brims were popular for summer (Figs 54, 58 and 98). Meanwhile, the cloth cap with a small peak was the most common style among ordinary working men and for country wear. The changing style of the cap may also aid closer dating of photographs: at the beginning of the century the cap was round and very neat, fitting the head closely (Fig. 54), but after around 1905 it grew larger and often appears rather wide in photographs of the 1910s (Fig. 55). Naturally, family photographs of younger men in civilian dress are uncommon during the war years, but many military images survive, as demonstrated in Chapter 12.

**56. Snapshot, late 1920s.** Menswear altered subtly during the 1920s. During and after the First World War low-cut shoes gradually replaced boots and trousers gained creases and turn-ups. Soft felt hats with a dented crown, like the trilby, became increasingly fashionable.

## 1920s

For much of the 1920s men usually appear in photographs wearing a fairly slim-fitting three-piece lounge suit, a slender cut the main feature that distinguishes this decade from later eras (Figs 56 and 94). Usually, the 1920s jacket had long lapels and with sombre business suits the traditional watch chain may still be seen, looped across the waistcoat front, although the wristwatch was now the modern method of keeping time. For most of the decade trousers appear rather narrow and short hemlines may reveal old-fashioned laced boots or, more commonly now, the modern low-cut shoe (Figs 56 and 94). For casual wear, a sports jacket and flannel trousers were becoming popular, 'flannels' often light-coloured for summer (Fig. 7). Various styles of neckwear occur in 1920s photographs, usually reflecting the age, status and taste of the wearer: occasionally a high standing or winged collar is worn and bow ties remained common for formal wear (Fig. 94); however, the usual everyday style was a modern-looking, softer (lightly starched or un-starched) turned down collar with sharp points, worn with the familiar knotted tie (Figs 7, 56, 94 and 107). Many older men were now clean-shaven, although some retained a neat moustache. Headwear was very diverse: the bowler was still correct for city business wear, while the cloth cap remained popular, especially with working men (Fig. 107); meanwhile, semi-casual fedora and trilby felt hats were increasingly fashionable (Fig. 56).

## 1930s

The cut of men's suits changed radically during the 1930s: some ultra-fashionable young men had adopted wide 'Oxford bags' during the mid–late 1920s and looser styles gradually entered mainstream fashion, as evidenced in 1930s photographs. Lounge jackets appear wider, shorter and rather boxy in cut, tailored with broad padded shoulders and sharp lapels, the suit trousers worn longer than previously and usually featuring prominent turn-ups (Fig. 38). In other respects, men's dress began to grow more relaxed during the 1930s, as seen in casual snapshots. Photographs may now show the lounge suit being worn without a waistcoat or with a knitted sleeveless pullover replacing the formal suit waistcoat, while for everyday wear some men discarded their ties, wearing their shirt collars wide open (Fig. 38). Sportswear was also developing: comfortable weekend flannels might be teamed with V-necked cricket-style jerseys (Fig. 64), while open-necked, short-sleeved sports shirts and even shorts were adopted for the first time, for outdoor leisure activities like walking, camping and cycling (Fig. 106). Some older men still sported a moustache during the 1930s (Fig. 95), although beards were now rare. Hats were often still worn in public – the wide cloth cap (Fig. 38), semi-formal felt trilby (Fig. 95) or perhaps a straw panama hat for summer.

## 1940s

Male fashion took a back seat during the Second World War as many men spent much of the decade in uniform (see Chapter 12). Few

**57. Snapshot, late 1940s.** During the 1930s and 1940s, suits were cut much looser than previously. Sports jackets were worn for casual wear, waistcoats were discarded and the shirt collar might be worn wide open over the jacket lapels. Men were usually clean-shaven.

acquired new civilian clothing during the war or throughout the period of rationing, while de-mob suits were often shapeless and lacked style. Therefore, in 1940s photographs men's jackets and trousers either appear rather loose and baggy (Fig. 57) or continue the generously cut tailored look of the 1930s (Figs 96 and 100). Sports jackets and trousers remained popular for weekend wear, usually worn without a waistcoat and often without a tie (Fig. 57). Checked jackets were common, as were striped and checked shirts. Any facial hair became distinctly unfashionable after the war, the neat toothbrush moustache formerly worn by some no longer favoured due to its associations with Hitler.

## Dating Children's Dress, 1840s–1940s
### Babies

As explained below in Chapter 6, in the early days of photography babies were photographed in the studio relatively rarely: more baby photographs survive for the late nineteenth century, although these are often christening or baptism portraits and the occasion is easily identifiable from the baby's long white gown (Fig. 71). Until around the First World War, male and female infants were usually dressed alike in white frocks and petticoats. Their appearance may be hard to date closely, unless fashionably dressed adults are also present in the scene.

It is useful to remember that in many picture collections, baby photographs date mainly from the twentieth century. In the Edwardian era 'best' baby wear for public display comprised impractical frilled, smock-like garments and wide 'halo' bonnets (Fig. 58). Conversely, it was also during the early 1900s and, especially, the 1910s that studio portraits began to portray semi-naked babies draped in blankets or wearing brief vest-like garments – a distinctive trend of the time (Fig. 59). When baby dresses are worn in photographs of the 1920s through to the 1940s, they are noticeably simpler in style and shorter than in early decades: knitted garments were also popular.

### Girls
#### 1840s–60s

In appearance, the clothing of Victorian daughters resembled that of their mothers, but until they came 'of age' they wore styles that expressed their youth. Between the 1840s and 1860s, essentially girls' garments were fashioned with a close-fitting bodice and full skirts (Fig. 60). Typically, little girls' dresses featured slit, boat-like necklines and short, puffed sleeves decorated with ribbon trimmings. Slightly older girls adopted gathered bodices and, often, tiered or flounced skirts, a shortened crinoline frame perhaps worn underneath and the hemline set below the knee or at low-calf level, depending

**58. Postcard, 1906.** Edwardian infants' 'Sunday best' wear was very ornate. This little boy wears a flounced summer frock and the wide 'halo' bonnet associated with the early 1900s.

**59. Postcard, early 1910s.** During the 1910s babies' and children's wear became less formal and the studio photo of a semi-naked baby, vest pulled down over one shoulder, became fashionable. This kind of picture is very rare before around 1910, so is relatively easy to date.

on their age (Fig. 60). Younger girls' hair was generally dressed in ringlets throughout the 1840s to 1860s, although their older sisters might wear more 'grown-up' styles that mirrored more closely ladies' coiffures.

### 1870s

During the early–mid 1870s, as women's outfits became layered and acquired a bustle behind the waist, so girls' garments broadly echoed the new style, comprising a short overdress or long tunic-style garment worn over a skirt, but without the adult bustle. Their hair, although still worn long in youthful mode, was drawn away from the face and dressed more ornately, following contemporary fashion. After mid-decade, as women's bodices lengthened and

**60.** *Carte de visite, c.* **1860.** Girls' frocks of the mid-nineteenth century followed contemporary female fashions for a fitted bodice and full skirt, the hemline lengthening as the girl grew older. Young girls wore long ringlets, while adolescents adopted more adult hairstyles.

a narrower line evolved, girls' styles followed this effect and typically consisted of a slender front-buttoning bodice and narrower skirt, as seen in Fig. 61. This image also shows how girls' hair followed fashion, often featuring the new fringe that came into vogue during the later 1870s, while black woollen stockings and leather button boots were the usual footwear.

## 1880s

Girls' photographs of the 1880s reveal frocks that are slender in style, the sleeves close-fitting or slightly puffed, bodices often gathered or pleated vertically down the centre and narrow skirts draped over the hips and pleated below, echoing contemporary female fashions (Fig. 31). As before, young girls did not adopt the second bustle, in vogue *c.* 1884–9, but their clothing followed the trend for contrasting fabrics, including velvet or plush, popular 1870s/1880s fabrics. The miniature sailor outfit also became fashionable during the 1880s, girls sometimes wearing a sailor-style white vest and blue blouse with striped collar, with a pleated skirt, even a sailor's hat (Fig. 68). Young girls continued to wear long hair loose, either styled with a short fringe or with the front hair drawn back (Figs 31 and 68).

## 1890s

By the turn of the 1890s, girls' dresses, still fairly narrow, were being secured around the waist with a wide fabric sash. Some toddlers wore a sash throughout the decade (Fig. 71), although a new smock dress had developed for girls by the mid-1890s – a loose garment fashioned with a flat yoke at the chest, onto which the length of the fabric was gathered and left to fall freely (Fig. 62). The comfortable smock-style frock with full sleeves is easily recognised and occurs often in photographs as it dominated girls' dress throughout the late-Victorian and Edwardian eras. Sailor-inspired features remained popular and a version of the sailor collar might be incorporated into the smock (Fig. 62). Hemlines extended below the knee during the later 1800s – a useful dating clue – while dark stockings and leather button boots remained the usual footwear.

## Early 1900s

The smock dress continued into the early 1900s as the mainstay of the young girl's wardrobe. A white smock, worn alone, could be ornamented with frills and flounces for 'Sunday best' (Fig. 37),

**61. *Carte de visite, c. 1876–80.*** Girls' dresses became slimmer during the later 1870s and 1880s, following adult styles. Black woollen stockings were worn with leather boots that usually fastened with buttons. A short fringe of hair became fashionable.

while plain, dark or coloured smocks were more practical for everyday and school wear, often being worn beneath a protective pinafore dress. In Edwardian photographs slightly older girls often wear a modified smock style, the dress (and pinafore, if worn) caught in at the waist, creating a more fitted, 'grown up' effect (Figs 37 and 141). For winter, dresses would be worn with black woollen stockings and boots fastening with traditional buttons or the more modern laces: for summer short white stockings (socks) might be teamed with coloured or white leather shoes. Prominent white hair bows became popular during the mid–late Edwardian era (Figs 37 and 141) and would continue throughout the following decade.

**62. Cabinet print,** *c.* **1896–9.** During the 1890s the loose smock dress was introduced for little girls and continued in use for the next twenty years or more. These smock dresses feature fashionable sailor-style collars. Dark woollen stockings and leather boots were still the norm.

## 1910s

Following wider female fashion trends, during the 1910s juvenile garments grew shorter and simpler in style, the frills and flounces of earlier decades becoming outmoded, although decorative broderie anglaise was fashionable for trimming hemlines (Fig. 118). Shorter versions of the traditional smock dress may occur in photographs of the early 1910s but as the loose smock grew outmoded, slimmer-fitting frocks became usual for young girls, made with a waist seam and, typically, a large collar, while hemlines rose to knee level, or higher for young girls. Winter-weight dresses sometimes featured ornamental buttons (then fashionable for ladies' skirts) and were usually teamed with dark stockings and leather boots (Fig. 122(b)). In summer, white cotton fitted dresses with long or three-quarter length sleeves were favoured, along with white socks and white or dark shoes (Fig. 118). Long hair was generally worn loose, or might be styled into ringlets accessorised with white bows, a late-Edwardian fashion that continued throughout the 1910s (Figs 118 and 122(b)). Young 'teenagers' usually wore knee-length dresses, drawn in at the waist, or separate blouses and skirts, with long stockings. For school wear a recognisable uniform was becoming established.

**63. Snapshot, dated 1920.** Girls' wear became much simpler during the 1910s and 1920s and hemlines grew shorter, to above the knee. Comfortable separates were popular by the 1920s and bare legs were common in summer. Hats were often worn, this example an early cloche style.

## 1920s

During the 1920s girls' clothing continued to grow simpler and more streamlined, hemlines now worn well above the knee. Following the general vogue for comfortable separates and knitwear, sweaters or jersey tops and skirts became fashionable (Fig. 63), while short-sleeved or sleeveless dresses in plain or patterned cotton material were popular for summer (Fig. 56). As spending time outdoors in the sunshine became more common (as explained later, in Chapter 11), increasingly we notice ankle socks or bare legs and bar shoes in snapshot photographs, although heads were usually protected in the sun by a brimmed hat (Figs 56 and 63). Young girls' hair might still be worn long, although often it was cut into a short bob, following fashion and offering another helpful dating clue (Fig. 140). Gymslips and blouses were the usual uniform for older school girls, some primary school girls also following suit (Fig. 140).

## 1930s and 1940s
Although simple shift-like dresses remained popular between the wars, photographs of the 1930s reveal a growing vogue for more ornamental, party-style dresses for young girls, influenced by the juvenile 'celebrities' of the day, child film star Shirley Temple and the royal princesses, Elizabeth and Margaret. Floral printed fabrics, frills, puffed sleeves and picturesque collars may all feature during this decade; hair may be short, although long hair was sometimes dressed in plaits, while wide-brimmed bonnets were popular for young girls (Fig. 64).

In general, dresses appear more shaped by the late 1930s and 1940s, usually made with a waist seam, short puffed sleeves and sometimes featuring a

**64. Snapshot, 1930s.** Men's and boys' weekend wear was becoming more relaxed during the 1930s. Although simple shift dresses remained popular for girls, party-style dresses with puffed sleeves were also fashionable.

**65. Walking picture, 1940s.** Girls' garments were rather tailored throughout the 1940s. Separate blouses and skirts were worn with blazer-style jackets or cardigans. Age differences were often expressed in hairstyles and footwear, although girls of all ages wore ankle socks.

gathered and smocked yoke. Everyday separates are also more common by the 1940s, a crisp blouse often worn with a knee-length A-line or pleated skirt, with a tailored blazer-style jacket or a more casual cardigan (Fig. 65). Knitwear was very popular during the 1930s and 1940s, ranging from cardigans and jerseys to outdoor hats, scarves and gloves. Still in the 1940s, before trousers and jeans became established in Britain for casual wear, older girls wore slightly longer hemlines than their younger sisters and usually dressed their hair in a shorter, more 'grown-up' style (Fig. 65).

## Boys

Just as Victorian and Edwardian girls were usually wearing adult dress by the age of 15 or 16, boys of the era had generally progressed to men's suits with long trousers and formal ties by their early–mid 'teens', or earlier, depending on their circumstances. The focus here is on recognising and dating the clothing worn by 'breeched' boys aged 3 or 4 and upwards, before they progressed to adult dress.

### 1840s and 1850s

Photographs of children taken during the 1840s and 1850s, before the main boom in photography, are rare, but when they do occur young boys' appearance echoes that of their mothers as much as that of their fathers. The usual young boy's outfit of the mid-nineteenth century was a thigh or knee-length tunic or dress featuring a fitted bodice and full skirt, similar to women's and girls' garments. Generally, wide trousers or knee-length drawers were worn underneath the dress or tunic, identifying the wearers firmly as boys, for girls never wore trousers or 'shorts' at that date.

**66. *Carte de visite*, early 1860s.** In the 1860s knickerbocker suits were devised for small boys who had been 'breeched'. Here is a *zouave* ensemble, a short bolero jacket, waistcoat and knickerbockers set, popular during the 1860s. Stockings might be striped at this time.

## 1860s and 1870s

The picturesque knee-length belted tunic or dress, worn with trousers, may sometimes occur in photographs of the early 1860s, although during this decade young boys' attire received a major make-over and a more masculine outfit was introduced. Typically, the new ensemble featured a short waist- or hip-length jacket, worn over a shirt, and teamed with short trousers called knickerbockers, that were either gathered or left open just below the knee. A popular early version of this style, often seen in 1860s photographs, was the *zouave* costume: this comprised a short bolero-style jacket with rounded front edges, worn with a waistcoat beneath and matching or contrasting knickerbockers (Fig. 66). Sometimes little boys' *zouave* suits were decorated with bold embroidery or braid, or else a plainer suit might be teamed with bright striped stockings. Throughout the 1860s and 1870s photographs demonstrate a variety of jacket and knickerbockers combinations for young boys. With velvet and plush fabrics becoming increasingly fashionable, during the 1870s a favourite 'Sunday best' outfit was the blouson-style velvet jacket worn with slender knickerbockers (Fig. 67).

**67. *Carte de visite*, c. 1876–7.** Boys' knickerbocker suits grew narrower in the late 1870s, following the lines of adult male and female fashion. Velvet and plush (cotton velvet) were popular fabrics.

## 1880s

By the later 1870s and early 1880s boys' dress was very diverse. On the one hand it was becoming plainer and more uniform, echoing the growing sobriety of contemporary menswear: for example, school boys' attire was developing into a sober dark jacket worn with knickerbockers or long trousers, depending on age; often this was teamed with the starched white collar known as the 'Eton collar' and a bow tie or long knotted tie (Fig. 68). Yet, conversely, various picturesque costumes were devised for small boys during the 1880s. The sailor suit came into vogue at this time and in the 1880s was often a copy of authentic naval uniform, complete with white vest, dark-blue blouse with a striped sailor collar and a sailor's cap (Fig. 68). Also popular for small boys, un-breeched or breeched, were fanciful velvet costumes with lace collars, accessorised with headwear that might have historical, Highland or naval influences (Figs 30 and 73).

**68. Early amateur snapshot, *c.* 1888.** Sailor suits first became fashionable for young boys and girls during the 1880s and only finally grew outmoded in the 1920s. The older brother, left, wears the late-Victorian schoolboy's outfit of jacket, trousers, shirt with Eton collar and knotted tie.

**69. School photograph, Odiham, Kent, early 1900s.** Young Edwardian school boys wore various jackets with cloth knickerbockers, dark woollen stockings and boots. A lounge jacket or Norfolk jacket with vertical stitched-down pleats and cloth belt were often worn with an Eton collar and silk bow or tie.

## 1890s and early 1900s

Sailor-inspired suits remained fashionable throughout the late-Victorian and Edwardian eras. Various loose blouse-style shirts, worn without a jacket, also appeared as casual boys' holiday and play wear, younger boys wearing prominent collars ranging from the sailor style to ornate wide frilled collars. Meanwhile, smarter cloth knickerbocker suits were evolving for 'Sunday best' and for slightly older boys to wear to school, with woollen stockings and leather boots (Fig. 69). For example, the distinctive Norfolk jacket, characterised by a fabric belt and vertical stitched-down pleats, entered the young boy's wardrobe during the 1890s, remaining a popular style until the 1910s and often worn with a starched Eton collar for school. An alternative style was the male lounge jacket with lapels, again worn with knickerbockers, this jacket usually teamed with a regular shirt and knotted tie: both styles are seen in Fig. 69.

## 1910s

Formal knickerbocker suits, worn with thick dark stockings, boots and a cloth cap outdoors, continued into the 1910s, especially for older boys. Simultaneously, many young boys were adopting a belted tunic and above-the-knee shorts set, tailored from woollen cloth (Fig. 122(b)). Sailor suits were sometimes worn on special occasions, for example to weddings, although they were beginning to grow outmoded and would disappear after the First World War. Progressive ideas about children's needs and a growing emphasis on practical play clothes also helped to popularise stretchy knitted jersey garments during this decade. Casual sweaters had been common wear among poorer children since at least the beginning of the century; however, only in the 1910s do studio photographs begin to portray small boys from 'respectable' families wearing the soft, comfortable jersey and shorts set, with socks and shoes or boots (Fig. 118).

## 1920s–40s

After the war, the knitted jersey with a small integral collar became a mainstay of young boys' wardrobes: worn throughout the 1920s–40s for general play and for elementary school (where regulation uniform was not always required), often the jersey incorporated a knitted tie (Fig. 140). For older boys, school uniform consisting of flannel shorts, shirt and tie, jacket or blazer and cloth cap or rounded school cap

**70. Snapshot, dated 1929.** A blazer or tailored jacket, above-the-knee shorts, shirt and grey socks often served as both school uniform and home clothes for boys between the 1920s and 1940s. Leather lace-up shoes were smart footwear, white canvas plimsolls for casual wear.

was well established by the 1920s (Fig. 99): the look, completed by grey socks and laced leather shoes or white canvas plimsolls, continued throughout the 1920s–40s and beyond. During this period, elements of boys' school uniform and everyday clothing were interchangeable, so in family photographs school-age boys often wear shirts and grey shorts, with or without ties and with or without tailored jackets or blazers as weekend wear (Fig. 70). Knitted garments were also popular, so sweaters and sleeveless pullovers of plain, cable or Fair Isle knit may also occur in photographs of these decades (Fig. 64).

*Part Two*

# STUDYING FAMILY PHOTOGRAPHS

# *Chapter 6*

# PROFESSIONAL PORTRAITS: IDENTIFYING THE OCCASION

To appreciate fully our photographs and understand how they connect to the family's history, we should consider *why* they may have been taken. What prompted that formal portrait depicting ancestors rigged out in 'Sunday best' dress? Historically, the paintings that pre-dated photographs were often commissioned to mark a special event and when photography became the new portrait medium in the mid-nineteenth century, commercial studios readily embraced themes that were already familiar and rapidly extended their repertoires. Various rites of passage, achievements and significant occasions prompted forebears from many walks of life to pose before the camera: christening or baptism, birthday, breeching, coming of age, educational or professional achievement, engagement, marriage, wedding anniversary, emigration, retirement and even death. It was not necessary, or common, for a photographer to be present at the event: by the turn of the century more professional operators were visiting client's homes, but generally the family member(s) involved in the occasion would visit their local photographer on the day, or around the time that it occurred, dressed in their best attire or in the most appropriate clothing. The resulting images, formally posed in an impersonal studio, were, inevitably, removed from reality, yet what was of most importance to our ancestors was the fact that they symbolised the significance of the occasion within the family. Special pictures shared with relatives, friends and neighbours, besides triggering personal recollections for years to come, enhanced the family's reputation, demonstrating visibly their good fortune, success, respectability and social status, and also testified to their correct observance of contemporary social ritual.

Once we understand that particular occasions may well have inspired many surviving professional portraits, we can look at our inherited family photographs afresh. What may initially appear standard images of forebears posing in a conventional studio setting can reveal a specific purpose, once they are closely examined. For example, some rituals entailed the wearing of designated forms of dress, such as mourning attire – clothes and accessories that have no place in our modern world, yet often recognisable in photographs. Some images offer little clear evidence of the circumstances that prompted them, but if the identity of the subject is already known or suspected, close dating of the picture using the techniques explained in Part One may reveal that the family member in question would have been celebrating a special birthday or landmark wedding anniversary at around that time. Equally, spotting a likely occasion in a photograph can sometimes aid closer dating, even identification of ancestors whose names had not previously been established. During the twentieth century increasingly personal and family events were recorded in amateur snapshots, although professional photographs were often favoured for key celebrations such as weddings and other special commemorative portraits. Below we consider the main social customs and family occasions observed in the past, suggesting how they may be identified in surviving photographs and offering representative pictorial examples.

## Christening and Baptism

One of the most momentous family events is the birth of a new baby and this was a regular occurrence in many households until smaller families became more common in the twentieth century. Despite the frequency of babies' births, relatively few Victorian and Edwardian photographs recording christenings and baptisms exist. Perhaps this is because wriggling babies were difficult to photograph, especially using the slower collodion process of the 1850s–70s; being too young to sit up unaided, newborn or tiny babies had to be held by a parent or nanny, or, if photographed alone, were supported on a couch or chair and secured firmly with sashes and scarves. If the prospect of this nerve-wracking experience didn't deter parents from taking their newly christened babies to be photographed, it seems likely that most families simply could not afford a professional portrait to announce the christening of every new arrival. By comparison, twentieth-century snapshots of babies' christenings survive in far greater numbers than earlier studio photographs. Whatever their type, baptism and christening images provide an important visual record of a family member's formal introduction into the world.

Christening photographs are usually distinguishable from other pictures of infants by the very young appearance of the baby and, especially, by his or her clothing. Christening gowns were usually white by the Victorian period, symbolising purity and innocence, and they continued in use in the twentieth century. Typically they were extremely long, at least twice the length of the baby, and were made of fine muslin or the most delicate fabric that a family could afford (Fig. 71). The cost of a christening gown depended upon the quality of the material and the complexity and craftsmanship of its lace and embroidery, so a portrait of a baby in exquisitely ornamented robes was a

**71. Christening photograph, 1894.** Early christening and baptism photographs are identifiable by the baby's very long gown: he or she is often very young. Sadly, this baby died later the same year.

clear visual expression of a family's solvency and social status. Christening gowns sometimes had a powerful family association, perhaps having originally been hand-made at home and passed down the generations: to many, the sense of tradition and continuity was important, although by the early twentieth century new 'Christening Robes' could be purchased for just a few shillings. An ornate cap or bonnet and sometimes an elaborate carrying cape or cloak often completed the formal christening outfit. Boys and girls were dressed alike, so it can be impossible to tell the gender of an unidentified baby in a christening photograph.

## Birthday

Lively infants were not the easiest subjects for photographers to work with, yet some actively marketed this potentially lucrative side of their business. Affluent parents might visit the studio annually around the time of their offspring's birthday, to record their growth and development. Some commercial photographers produced 'Baby's Album', to encourage the collection and display of regular portraits of sons and daughters throughout their childhood and adolescence. Toys and novelties were kept in photographers' studios to engross young children during the sitting, so birthday photographs may show infants holding dolls or teddy bears, standing by prams or mounted on rocking horses. For ordinary working families with many children, the juvenile birthday photograph might be a rare indulgence, or perhaps it was more convenient and cost-effective if the birthday boys or girls were twins and the two could be pictured together, as in Fig. 62. Evidently, in some families birthday photographs were postponed until the more auspicious 21st birthday portrait, when a son or daughter officially attained adulthood.

The 21st birthday photograph occurs frequently in family picture collections, although it may not be immediately obvious. A studio portrait may simply represent a young adult wearing elaborate or fashionable clothing, so we can only judge their likely age

**72. Carte de visite, c. 1883–5.**
Judging from the youthful appearance of this ancestor, this photograph may have been his 21st birthday portrait. This was an important occasion that often prompted young adults to visit the photographer, although it is hard to identify positively in photos.

and, if their identity is known and the time frame of the photograph fits, make an educated guess at the likely occasion (see, for example, Figs 29, 32, 52 and 72). Sometimes he or she wears a floral corsage or buttonhole in honour of the event and in the case of female subjects it is worthwhile looking out for jewellery items such as gold brooches or lockets that may have been presented as a special 21st birthday gift: these kinds of heirlooms have often been kept and passed down the generations. Older family members also celebrated landmark birthdays, as seen in Figs 2, 8 and 10. It was especially common for the elderly to commemorate 60th, 70th and even later birthdays with a photograph demonstrating their good health and longevity. Sometimes the occasion may have been recorded or remembered within the family, but otherwise again we have to judge whether a well-dressed ancestor or relative portrayed (usually) in a single photograph may have been celebrating a special birthday.

## Breeching

After christening and early birthdays, the next significant event in a little boy's life was his 'breeching', a rite of passage no longer recognised today but an important family and social ritual that historically marked a son's transition from infancy into boyhood. Small children of both sexes wore baby dresses in the nineteenth and early twentieth centuries, but at some point between the age of 3 and 6 – usually at 4 or 5 – boys relinquished their androgynous baby robes and were ceremoniously dressed in their first pair of short trousers or knickerbockers. In recognition of their new status, lucky boys were often given pennies by relatives and neighbours and in some families the occasion was recorded in a professional photograph. Surviving breeching portraits are sometimes annotated on the back with the boy's name, age and the date; otherwise a breeching photograph is generally clear from the appearance of the subject - a small boy aged around 4 or thereabouts, posing usually alone

**73. Breeching cabinet print, 1890s.** Victorian breeching photographs occur often in family picture collections as the breeching of sons was an important rite of passage. Usually, the boy was about 4 years old and was photographed wearing his new knickerbocker suit.

(Figs 66, 67 and 73), but occasionally with a sibling who may have been celebrating a birthday at the same time. Typically, the young son modelled his new set of 'grown-up' clothes – garments made in the prevailing style for young boys: for example, in the 1860s a boy often adopted the new *zouave* ensemble on the occasion of his breeching (Fig. 66), while picturesque velvet knickerbockers costumes were in vogue between the 1870s and 1890s (Figs 67 and 73). This exclusively male tradition explains the large number of photographs of small boys that survive: the breeching ritual continued until around the First World War, later in some families.

## Coming of Age

For girls there was no equivalent of young boys' breeching, but as they grew older their dress hemlines steadily lengthened from knee, to calf, to ankle and their clothing became progressively more 'grown up' in its style and construction. Finally, at some point broadly between the ages of 15 and 18, often at around 16, a girl came 'of age': this important rite of passage was

**74.** *Carte de visite, c.* **1890–2.**
This ancestor was born in 1874, so her photograph, dateable to *c.* 1890–2, may represent her 'coming of age' portrait when she was aged 16–18 years old. The point at which a girl adopted full adult fashions was a notable event, a century or more ago.

expressed in the adoption of full adult dress – a firmly fitted corset, floor-length skirts with a crinoline or bustle support (if fashionable) and the putting up of long hair into a neat bun or chignon. In some families the transition was marked by a special photograph, as seen in Fig. 74. It can be difficult to identify positively coming of age photographs, but formal portraits of female ancestors who appear to be aged in around their mid-'teens' may well have been taken for that purpose. As with many old traditions, the ritual declined after the First World War, by which time simpler female fashions rendered it redundant: dress continued to reflect girls' age differences, but in more subtle ways.

## Academic and Vocational Success

Some photographs of youthful ancestors and relatives may celebrate academic attendance and achievement. When children left school or attained a recognised standard of education, it was common for them to be presented with a certificate and sometimes this was recorded in a special photograph. For those who undertook higher education often a special photograph would be

**75. Postcard portrait, c. 1907–9.** This relative was just a youth in this studio photograph but he wears a smart business suit and sits reading a newspaper. It is the kind of formal portrait that may well record his entry into the workplace or an important new job.

taken to mark the commencement of a course, or their graduation. Similarly, other young people might pose for a photograph to record their embarkation on a technical college course or vocational training programme, or on its successful completion. At times of war new recruits into the armed forces and other services were often photographed in uniform, as discussed in Chapter 12. An ancestor's first full-time job, commencement of a new career, promotion to a new position or a notable success at work might also prompt a visit to the studio, as may well have been the case in Fig. 75. Where special occupational dress or a uniform was required, this was proudly modelled in the picture – a theme explored further in Chapter 11.

## Engagement

In the past, the length of a young couple's engagement depended on various factors including their family circumstances and their ages. In many families evidently the engagement period was brief, progressing swiftly to marriage, especially during war or if the woman was already pregnant, while more formal engagements might last between six months and two or more years.

**76. Engagement** *carte de visite*, **early 1880s.** A daughter's engagement inspired a special commemorative portrait in some families, especially by the late nineteenth century. The young woman would display her engagement ring prominently, as seen clearly here.

Where an engagement was recognised as a distinct event in its own right, it was often marked by a special photograph, especially in the later Victorian and Edwardian eras. A betrothed couple might be pictured together in the photographer's studio or in separate portraits that were then exchanged; however, evidence suggests that young ladies were especially keen to demonstrate their new status in a photograph, a copy of which might be given as a romantic token to their fiancé. A formal engagement involved the prospective bridegroom presenting a ring to his intended, an expression of his provision of security for the completion of the bargain, this custom growing more common by the late nineteenth century, when jewellery became more affordable for ordinary people. The ring was therefore highly symbolic, visible proof of the occasion, and, accordingly, in engagement photographs the woman prominently displays the new ring (Fig. 76).

## Marriage

Marriages are perhaps the most special of all family occasions and nearly all family historians possess wedding photographs in their collections: some will be of nineteenth-century origins, although the marriage portraits of our ordinary Victorian ancestors may well go unidentified because the special

**77. Wedding photograph, c. 1900.** The familiar 'white wedding' took decades to become established as the norm throughout society: many of our Victorian and Edwardian ancestors simply visited the photographer's studio after the wedding, wearing their best clothes, as seen here.

white bridal wear, bouquets, flowers and bridesmaids that we tend to associate with weddings are often absent (Fig. 77). By the early twentieth century many more family weddings were 'white weddings', more recognisable to the modern eye. Marriage occasions – and the photographs in which they were recorded – varied enormously, reflecting different families' circumstances and the eras in which they lived. Because of their popularity and diversity, we examine wedding photographs separately in Chapter 10.

## Wedding Anniversary

Since at least the Middle Ages, milestone twenty-fifth (silver) and fiftieth (golden) wedding anniversaries have been observed, but it was not until the Victorian era that the ritual and celebration surrounding the 'anniversary wedding', as it was then called, were redefined and popularised throughout Western society. Sources of information concerning the celebration of wedding anniversaries vary in their details, but collectively they suggest that

**78. Possible wedding anniversary portrait, early 1900s.** Photographs of older couples often occur in family picture collections and in many cases the occasion was a landmark twenty-fifth, thirtieth, fortieth or even fiftieth wedding anniversary.

by the turn of the twentieth century around nine principal wedding anniversaries were officially recognised: first, fifth, tenth, fifteenth, twentieth, twenty-fifth, fiftieth, sixtieth and seventieth. Photographic evidence certainly supports a growing trend towards celebration of several key anniversaries by the time of our late-Victorian and Edwardian ancestors and suggests that some couples may have formally commemorated every fifth wedding anniversary. Sometimes photographs marking landmark anniversaries are identified, but in many cases the occasion may not be immediately obvious and requires a firm date range for the image, as well as a degree of personal judgement. Sometimes the anniversary couple pose on their own in the studio or perhaps at home in the garden, one person usually standing while their spouse is seated (Fig. 78): in other images they are   seated, surrounded by their children and any grandchildren, making the occasion more of a family celebration.

## Mourning

Extravagant mourning customs date back centuries in Europe but, like many other social rituals, public mourning became more pronounced and widespread during the nineteenth century. By the 1850s ostentatious funerals and the wearing of prescribed mourning attire were well established among the middle and upper classes, and the mourning industry, including undertakers and specialist outfitters, was positively booming. After the untimely death of Prince Albert in 1861, Queen Victoria adopted a sombre public image and wore black and half-mourning colours for the rest of her life, appearing to her subjects as the epitome of Christian widowhood. Thus, under royal influence the growing cult of mourning gained mass appeal in Victorian Britain, and throughout the British Empire.

Families being generally much larger and the average life expectancy significantly lower in the past, compared with today, the passing of loved ones of all ages occurred frequently and were only too familiar experiences. Lengthy public mourning following the death of a relative, close friend or an important public figure reached a height between the 1860s and 1890s, although the custom continued into the Edwardian era and, in some families, throughout the 1910s. By then, the strictest rules governing mourning had already relaxed, and after the First World War, which had witnessed death on an unimaginable scale and caused many to question their religious beliefs, extended public mourning became unfashionable, except among royalty and the upper classes, and, conversely, some poorer communities. Eventually, public mourning became one of many outmoded social customs, but the importance of visibly mourning the deceased was once firmly entrenched in the lives of our forebears.

Mourning and mourning dress is a complicated subject that requires a more detailed explanation than is possible here: for further information, Lou

**79. Mourning** *carte de visite, c.* **1870.** This ancestor was not wealthy, but she sat for a special mourning photograph following the death of her husband in April 1870. Her outfit and bonnet are made of very dull matt-black mourning fabric and her cuffs are trimmed with bands of crape.

Taylor's *Mourning Dress* (George Allan & Unwin, 1983) is recommended. Mourning conduct and the wearing of mourning attire were governed by labyrinthine and ever-changing 'rules', advice being promulgated in the etiquette manuals and domestic handbooks that proliferated from the mid-nineteenth century onwards. Essentially, the nature and length of mourning depended upon the relationship of the mourner to the deceased, but over time mourning dress specifications became more intricate and the prescribed mourning periods longer, the tendency for different published sources to vary only adding to the complexity of the custom. In its heyday critics denounced both the unnecessary pressure under which the requirement to wear special mourning clothing placed poor families and the excessive luxury and display that it encouraged among the upper classes. Clearly, only the prosperous could afford to follow every recommendation down to the last detail, but family photographs reveal that our humbler ancestors also adopted mourning as far as they could: to be seen correctly following social etiquette was important to most respectable Victorian families (Figs 79 and 80).

A formal studio portrait portraying the bereaved adorned in suitable mourning attire was a significant aspect of the ritual and many of today's family historians will discover mourning photographs in their archives. Ancestors may be wearing mourning dress in early daguerreotypes and ambrotypes and from the 1860s onwards this became a common theme of popular *carte de visite* photographs and cabinet prints. Mourning pictures take many forms, ranging from single or double portraits to larger family groups, for mourning affected everyone – men, women and children. However, female mourning photographs are by far the most common. Women carried the heaviest burden, particularly widows, who were officially supposed to mourn their husbands for at least two-and-a-half years, although many older widows never wore colours again but retained sombre black dress throughout their remaining years.

Mourning dress largely followed fashion, so mourning photographs are dateable from the basic style of garments and hairstyles, much like other images. Firmly identifying the occasion requires recognising the dress details that specifically signified mourning: these may be quite obvious in some photographs, less clear in others. Essentially, black garments were adopted for the early stages of mourning, small amounts of white sometimes being introduced, for example in a blouse collar or cuffs (Fig. 80). However, since sedate dark or black clothing was commonly favoured by older Victorian and Edwardian ladies, it may be unclear whether an ancestor is in mourning or simply dressed according to her age and personal taste. One identifying feature of mourning dress was that, officially, nothing was supposed to shine or gleam, so shimmering silks were discouraged and garments were usually fashioned from matt-black materials like bombazine (worsted and silk material) and paramatta (worsted and cotton). Although the precise quality of fabrics is not always discernible in photographs, sometimes materials with a very dull appearance can be identified and generally they indicate mourning attire, as seen in Figs 79 and 80. Even more obvious is black crêpe (or *crape*) – a crimped, dull silk gauze fabric recognisable from its distinctive textured appearance: crape could be used to cover whole garments for First or Deep mourning, although it was often limited to panels and modest trimmings (Fig. 79). Mourning specifications also included ornaments and accessories, so chunky jewellery of jet or cheaper black materials often replaced gold trinkets. Further indications of female mourning may include black clothing worn with a special headdress: headwear took various forms, ranging from a modest black bonnet tied under the chin (Fig. 79) to a cap or hat displaying a veil or long fabric 'falls' (streamers), as in Fig. 80.

Male mourning dress was far simpler than women's attire and by the photographic era usually required a black suit worn with a black tie, although sometimes a watch chain fashioned from a dull black metal was adopted and, occasionally, a black armband. Children were also put into black clothes if, for example, they had lost a parent or sibling; many thought it inappropriate for infants to wear black, so instead toddlers might be dressed in white garments with black trimmings. Once a mourning portrait has been identified, it is often possible to connect it to within a year or two of a recorded death in the family, especially if the identity of the subject(s) is already known, since they were probably closely related to the deceased. A closely dated photograph firmly linked to mourning may even assist with identifying a forebear who has not yet been named, as the occasion will narrow down the possibilities.

**80. Mourning photograph, 1898.** This photograph was taken at the widow's home in September 1898, her husband having died in December 1897. She wears touches of white, but otherwise her outfit and cap with falls are fashioned from the dull-black fabric required for mourning.

## Family Groups

Group photographs picturing several members of the same family were always a popular subject. During the nineteenth and early twentieth centuries great emphasis was placed on the importance of family life and middle-class Victorian values are clearly expressed in many family group scenes. A visual demonstration of the traditional household hierarchy might be conveyed by a patriarchal father presiding over a gathering of his wife and offspring, or the special joys of motherhood evoked in a picturesque scene depicting the woman of the family with her children (Fig. 31). The 'generations' photograph was also popular, portraying members of three or four generations together, celebrating the healthy progression and continuation of the family line. Sometimes a family group signified the imminent departure of one of their number, perhaps the emigration of family members overseas, or military deployment in times of war, as explained in Chapter 12.

## Post-mortem Photographs

Occasionally Victorian families commissioned photographs of relatives just after they had passed away, marking the final rite of passage. The deceased was usually portrayed in repose on a couch or in bed, with eyes closed peacefully, as though sleeping. This genre of historical photography generates a certain morbid interest today and many photographs posted online are described as post-mortem pictures, when they are clearly not. Genuine post-mortem photographs survive only rarely in British family picture collections. When they do occur, most examples depict babies or small children who tragically died before their time, or elderly ancestors (Fig. 81).

**81. Post-mortem ambrotype,** *c.* **1862.** This re-touched ambrotype is a genuine post-mortem photograph, thought to represent an elderly ancestor who died in 1862. Usually in such pictures the deceased was photographed in repose, as if sleeping.

# Chapter 7

# PHOTOGRAPHIC COPIES

Once card-mounted photographic prints became common in the 1860s, it was possible to make printed copies of earlier images, whether an early one-off daguerreotype or ambrotype photograph, an existing *cdv* or, more rarely, a copy of a family painting dating from the pre-photographic era. The ability to produce copies or enlarged photographs was publicised by many studios on the backs of their mounts, along with other business information. If the image to be copied was a photograph (as was usually the case) and if the negative was still available, the new copy would be of higher quality than if it was created from a photographic print. However, if a long period of time elapsed between the taking of the original photograph and the making of the copy, the negative was less likely to be accessible and the reprint usually had to be made from the surviving photograph.

## Enlargements

Sometimes a family member desired a larger, more imposing portrait than the usual small photograph and so would order a photographic enlargement that could be framed and hung on the wall at home. This might occur at the time of the original photograph sitting or soon afterwards, or it perhaps was several decades before a son or daughter decided that they would like a substantial picture of a parent to keep and display. Enlargements can be virtually any size, although life-sized head and shoulders portraits are perhaps most common. Partly because visual detail could be lost in the enlarging process, and also in the interests of creating a more attractive, life-like representation, enlargements were very often enhanced, using oil or watercolour paints or crayons. Sometimes the colour re-touching was so heavy that the resulting picture looks more like a painting than a photograph, causing some doubt over the medium. Photographer details were not always included on enlargements and they can be hard to date as objects, but at least the image, whether heavily painted or still retaining its photographic quality, should be dateable from the details of dress.

## Photographic Copies

Sometimes several photographic copies were ordered from the photographer

**82. Copy photograph: memorial portrait.** This photographic print is clearly a copy of an earlier image: a memorial portrait. The *carte de visite* card mount dates to the mid-1860s, when W Boswell of Norwich made the copy, but fashion clues confirm that the original photograph was a 1840s daguerreotype.

at the time of the original sitting, so in a sense these count as multiple original photographs: extra card-mounted photographic prints were useful for presenting to friends and family members and were often ordered if a close relative was emigrating or going away to war, as discussed in Chapter 12. Sometimes copies were inspired by the acquisition of a new photograph album, for which uniform *carte* or cabinet-sized photographs were needed: a sister, wife or daughter might request copies of photographs of living relatives, to add to the growing album collection of family portraits. Equally, they might arrange reprints of earlier photographs of forebears who had passed away.

## Memorial Portraits

The most common kind of photographic copy to occur in today's family collections is the later reprint of an older photograph. This type of picture is most obvious when the visual image looks significantly earlier than the estimated age of the card mount and/or the photographer's operational dates. Further clues are a faint, diminished picture quality, and/or a neat vignette portrait presented in the middle of the mount, as seen in Fig. 82. Sometimes the copy photograph is very small: such diminutive portraits were often intended to be cut out and mounted in a piece of personal jewellery, such as a locket. When first encountered, copy photographs can be confusing, since the format, image, photographer details and mount style don't all accord with one another; however, major disparities between the various aspects of the picture are usually clear evidence of a reprint of an earlier photograph.

Generally, when an earlier photograph was reprinted at a later date, it was what is termed a 'memorial portrait' – a copy photograph produced following the death of its subject. After a person had died, a close relative might organise copies of an existing photograph of him or her (taken from life), so that they, and perhaps other family members too, could each have a picture by which to remember the deceased. Usually, these memorial portraits were ordered from the relative's local photographer, whose details were often printed on their mount in the usual way. This identified them as the creator of the copy, *not* as the photographer who took the initial photograph: unfortunately, the name and studio address of the original photographer have usually become lost in the process. The copy photograph was presented in the format most popular at that time: for example, an original 1840s daguerreotype photograph or 1850s ambrotype photograph would usually be copied and printed in the 1860s onto a *carte de visite* mount, as in Fig. 82. Similarly, a *cdv* dating from the 1860s or 1870s might be copied later, in the 1890s or early 1900s, onto a fashionable cabinet-sized mount.

Some memorial portraits bear a helpful handwritten inscription on the back stating the name and date of death of the subject, although many do not carry this information. They do, though, present their own unique clues which can help to identify an unknown ancestor. First, judging the age of the subject and approximately dating the visual image should offer some idea of their approximate birth date: see Chapter 9 for tips on judging age. Evidence suggests that in many instances memorial portraits were created fairly soon after death – typically within a few years – so accurately dating the style of mount onto which the copy image has been printed should help with estimating the likely time frame of the subject's death. If a family member appears very youthful in the image, then there is a strong possibility that he or she died when young, for if they had lived a longer life a more recent photograph showing them when middle-aged or elderly is more likely to have been copied for the memorial portrait.

# Chapter 8

# INHERITED PHOTOGRAPH ALBUMS

Some family historians are fortunate in inheriting not only family photographs, but also old nineteenth or early twentieth-century photograph albums compiled by ancestors and more recent relatives. In this chapter we look at the history of photograph albums, how to identify albums from different eras and how to analyse their contents.

## Early Photograph Albums

As the neat *carte de visite* photograph became fashionable, inspiring the 'cartomania' craze, so the first purpose-designed photograph albums were produced, while the availability of albums in turn encouraged the taking and collection of more *carte de visite* photographs. In fact, during the early 1860s, *cdvs* were known as 'album portraits', demonstrating the close relationship between these popular photographic prints and the fashion for displaying them in the new albums. The first albums were produced in France, but they were available in Britain as early as the summer of 1861. Designed to look externally like the traditional family Bible or hymnal, early albums were stout volumes with heavy embossed leather bindings and sturdy metal clasps. As Audrey Linkman explains in *The Victorians: Photographic Portraits* (Tauris Parke, 1993), the conscious emulation of devotional books endowed the new photograph albums with something of the respect and awe accorded to the Christian religion in the Victorian age. The connection also implied that a collection of family photographs in a handsome book might even replace the existing custom of recording births, marriages and deaths inside family Bibles: one contemporary commentator even described the album as 'an illustrated book of genealogy'. From the mid-Victorian era onwards, the photograph album would become a treasured repository of all that a family held dear.

Elegant photograph albums, coveted and prestigious household possessions, soon became fashionable items in many middle-class homes. They made ideal Christmas and birthday presents, particularly for ladies, and some surviving albums bear hand-written inscriptions, naming the recipient, donor and the date of the gift – valuable recorded historical information. Early album owners were said to be delighted with the way in which the photographic cards could be arranged, in a manner that both preserved and displayed them. The main album pages were designed with pre-cut apertures for the convenient insertion and organisation of the prints, while inside the front cover sometimes a 'page one' *carte de visite* photograph was included – a frontispiece with verses addressed to family and friends about to view the album contents. By the 1880s special stands and holders for displaying albums on the mantelpiece or sideboard were becoming popular drawing room ornaments. The photograph album was not only an important family keepsake and domestic status symbol, but also provided a popular social diversion.

## Studying Victorian albums

Victorian photograph albums range in their proportions from small books displaying just one *carte de visite* photograph (measuring around 10cm x 6.5cm) per page, to significantly larger volumes designed to take two or even four *cartes* per page. The first albums of the 1860s and early 1870s feature

**83. Page from photograph album presented in 1886.** Late-Victorian photograph albums usually contain both *cdv* and cabinet-sized apertures. They were typically very ornate, as seen from the decorative painted surround framing this cabinet print.

only neat *carte*-sized apertures in their inside pages, since *cdvs* dominated portrait photography at that time; however, by the mid–late 1870s the larger cabinet photograph measuring around 16.5cm x 11.5cm (first introduced in 1866) was becoming fashionable, so from then onwards new albums tended to incorporate the two sizes of apertures, to accommodate both types of photograph. In view of this trend, the size of the apertures within an undated album can help with firmer dating of the volume. The styles of album bindings also changed over time, while their pages grew progressively elaborate as fashionable taste inclined increasingly towards the ornate: in many late-Victorian albums apertures were decoratively framed with watercolour paintings, as seen in Fig. 83. Photograph albums, like photographs themselves, gradually reduced in price and eventually became affordable for more ordinary families. Special albums also began to be produced, for example, albums for babies and children and, apparently, for post-mortem portraits, although they are rare in Britain. The special wedding photograph album, purchased by the bride and filled with photographs of the wedding party and officiating clergyman, also came into vogue and was said to be highly fashionable by the late 1880s.

## The Album Contents

Photograph album collections were often (though not always) commenced by a woman, since it was usually the lady of the house who preserved the family photographs and other records. Afterwards the album would be carefully passed down through the family, often to female descendants. The vast majority of photographs inside – if not all of them – were professional studio portraits, since few of our ancestors were engaging in amateur photography during the nineteenth century. Sometimes earlier photographs dating from before the album was acquired were displayed inside, while ensuing generations might also add later portraits. Surviving Victorian albums may, then, include assorted photographs that span at least four decades, from the 1860s to the 1890s or early 1900s, although in many cases most of the photographs will date to within about the first ten or fifteen years of the album's origins. Ancestors' names have sometimes been written on the album pages beneath the photographs: this manuscript information may or may not be accurate. As with any historical 'evidence', it is important to try to verify the details, by dating the photographs (or having them dated) as closely as possible: unfortunately, sometimes names were added to an album by a later family member who did not personally know the subjects and was merely guessing at their identities and this can be very misleading.

Sometimes it is necessary temporarily to remove photographs from their apertures to study any printed studio information on the back and perhaps to scan them, but afterwards they should be returned to their original positions within the album. The arrangement of photographs inside an album may appear random, but the layout can sometimes offer significant clues. There was usually a purpose to their organisation: for example, often the first image portrayed the album's original owner or a very close family member such as a parent or spouse; beyond that, paired portraits of husbands and wives were often displayed alongside each other and on the same or opposite pages were placed pictures of the couples' children, while photographs of other relatives might branch out further throughout the album. There were no precise rules, however, and of course the contents may have been subsequently rearranged by a later family member, but respecting the organisation of photographs within the album at the time it was inherited will at least preserve any connections once considered relevant: this should provide a helpful starting point for further research.

## Family Snapshot Albums

As discussed in Chapter 1, amateur family photography became popular during the early twentieth century and naturally snapshot albums survive in greater numbers today than do than weighty, leather-bound Victorian tomes. Snapshot albums originating between the early 1900s and 1920s are characteristically relatively modest paper- or cloth-covered volumes and may have been manufactured by one of the well-known photographic companies of the period, such as Kodak or Ogden's (Fig. 84). Their pages, formed of sturdy black or off-white card, often have pre-cut apertures designed to take the small snapshot prints measuring just a few centimetres that were typical of the era (Fig. 85). By the 1930s and 1940s, larger albums were becoming common, their pages often thinner and left plain so that prints of different sizes could be arranged inside, using adhesive corners. As with Victorian albums, twentieth-century snapshot albums were frequently given as Christmas or birthday presents so there may be a helpful inscription and date inside the front cover. Earlier photographs could be displayed in a new album, as seen in Fig. 85 (in which the central photograph pre-dates the album), especially where there was a long history of snapshot photography within the

**84. Ogden's snapshot photograph album, dated 1909.** Early twentieth-century snapshot albums were sometimes given as gifts and inscribed with the date. This example was produced by the photographic company Ogden's.

M.I.A. 1909?

Hurstbourne Tarrant
Father & Cousin. 1903

AT Norwood.

Margie. Norman. Constie.
1916.

**85. Page from 1909 album.** Edwardian snapshot albums often had pre-cut apertures, although earlier prints could be stuck on to the pages. This page has been annotated: the central photograph pre-dates the album, the others were taken later.

family; however, a carefully preserved snapshot album may coincide with the family's purchase of their first camera, in which case the year of a dated album indicates the earliest likely date for most of the snapshots within.

As with any inherited photograph album, when removing photographs from a snapshot album remember to replace them in their original positions as the picture sequence may be relevant. In particular, photographs displayed on the same and adjacent pages of snapshot albums can often help with dating and identification of scenes that are proving harder to analyse. Sometimes details such as names, the year and the location are recorded on the backs of snapshots, or on the album pages, as shown in Fig. 85. These handwritten notes are likely to be more reliable than the names written in Victorian albums, since the author was very often the photographer or someone in the snapshot. Other photographs may be unmarked and perhaps present baffling images of unfamiliar people or places that appear to offer few clues, yet patient research and further investigation often yields a better understanding of these snapshots. Being relatively recent images, twentieth-century snapshots may well be identifiable by someone else in the family, especially if taken within living memory, so it is well worth showing snapshot albums to relatives, particularly members of the older generation: photographs often trigger recollections and help with making visual connections. Another family member may even have copies of the same snapshots, or similar views that were annotated on the back and can therefore shed light on our own photographs.

## Chapter 9

# JUDGING STATUS, AGE AND LIKENESS

An accurate date range can always be established for family photographs using the various photograph dating techniques explained earlier in this book, and we have looked at the kinds of important occasions that often prompted ancestors and relatives to commission a photograph, but what else might we learn about earlier generations by studying their images? The questions that commonly occur in this connection include: whether a person's or a family's appearance in a photograph reveals anything of their social status; what kind of age they look to be; and how we might spot similarities or resemblances between the subjects of the same or different photographs.

### Family Photographs and Social Status

Sometimes researchers wonder whether we can determine anything about forebears' social or economic status from their likenesses: is there anything about their appearance that indicates whether they were especially poor, or fairly prosperous. Usually, family historians have formed some idea of ancestors' occupational and social background, although, as we know, in the nineteenth and early twentieth centuries, before the welfare state provided aid for those in reduced circumstances, family fortunes could fluctuate dramatically. Therefore, the economic position of earlier generations may well be reflected in the number and nature of photographic portraits in which they are portrayed.

As suggested in Chapter 5 when we considered dress in photographs, our most impoverished family members are unlikely to have ever visited a commercial studio, or perhaps only when deemed absolutely essential: for example, the elderly ancestor of humble status pictured in Fig. 79 only appears in this one photograph from a vast family picture archive – a formal mourning portrait following the death of her husband, taken at the height of Victorian mourning customs. Conversely, some ordinary working ancestors who might not be expected to have been photographed very frequently may surprise us by appearing in many portraits: for instance, the young domestic servant seen in Figs 74 and 87 is pictured in at least seven separate *cdv* and cabinet portraits

If posting
from outside
of the UK
please affix
stamp here

Pen & Sword Books

FREEPOST SF5

47 Church Street

BARNSLEY

South Yorkshire

S70 2BR

# DISCOVER MORE ABOUT HISTORY

**Pen & Sword Books** now offer over 3,000 titles in print covering all aspects of history including Military, Maritime, Aviation, Local, Family, Transport, Crime, Political and soon Social History. We also do books on nostalgia and have now introduced a range of military DVD's and Historical Fiction. If you would like to receive our catalogues and leaflets on new books and offers, please fill in the details below and return this card (no postage required).

Alternatively, register online at www.pen-and-sword.co.uk.

(Please note: we do not sell data information to any third party companies).

Visit www.WarfareMagazine.co.uk for free military history content including commemorative anniversary articles, military news, reviews, competitions and new product releases.

Title ......... Name.................................................................

Address....................................................................................

.............................................................. Postcode.....................

Email Address .........................................................................

If you wish to receive our email newsletter, please tick here

**Website: www.pen-and-sword.co.uk • Email: enquiries@pen-and-sword.co.uk**
**Telephone: 01226 734222 • Fax: 01226 734438**

**86. *Carte de visite*, 1863.** Images of prosperous ancestors are often evident from their lavish clothing and from the ornate studio setting. This photograph was taken by the Southwell Brothers of Baker Street, who photographed royalty and the social elite.

taken between 1890 and 1897, when she was aged 16–23, wearing a completely different outfit in every photograph. We all spend our earnings in different ways, some more visible than others: a century or more ago young single working men and women who enjoyed wearing stylish outfits probably splashed out on more studio portraits than their elders, who had other financial responsibilities, or who perhaps felt that they had little to display in a picture.

It can sometimes be hard to judge social status or financial position very precisely from formal studio photographs since even humble ancestors usually donned their smartest, most fashionable clothing when they had their photograph taken. However, while the ordinary working population could generally follow the basic styles that were in vogue at a particular time, few women could have afforded – or would have had the need for – the most luxurious fabrics and costly and extravagant accessories or garment trimmings. Therefore, when we encounter a photograph of a female ancestor dressed in an ornate ensemble, as in Fig. 86, or in shimmering silk materials profusely embellished with lace (Fig. 42), this would generally imply a lady of privileged or relatively affluent status. The same general principle applies to male portraits, which may stand out because of the elegant cut and fit of the subject's garments, his stylish accessories and the nonchalant pose of one with an innate sense of self-confidence (Fig. 29).

Studio settings may also contribute to the superior image conveyed in professional photographs depicting well-heeled ancestors. Prestigious portrait photographers patronised by royalty, aristocracy and the upper and upper-middle classes predictably charged higher prices for their portraits, but provided luxurious facilities and some of the most elaborate studio settings of their day, as seen in Figs 29 and 86. By contrast, inexpensive high-street studios catering for a humbler clientele operated more basic premises with fewer props and plainer sets. With outdoor photographs, social status and relative prosperity become even more obvious, since family members are portrayed in natural surroundings that usually reflect their living conditions and lifestyles: compare, for example, the spacious, elegant settings of Figs 39, 97 and 98 with the cramped gardens of Figs 37, 91 and 100.

## Estimating Age in Family Photographs

Estimating the likely age of an ancestor or relative represented in an old black and white photograph can be challenging, although we all attempt this at some point, perhaps in order to work out the subject's identity, or, if identity is already known, to establish at what stage of life they were portrayed. Judging age accurately is difficult, for several reasons: humans tend to age at varying rates and in slightly different ways and, in addition, sometimes they have sought to disguise the passage of time through artifice, creating a more youthful impression. Another factor is that many old photographs display very small faces that reveal little, if any, real detail. Images may also be imperfect, faded or over-exposed, adding to the difficulty of gaining a true sense of facial characteristics. In addition, one viewer's opinion concerning appearance and age may differ quite significantly from that of another: we all see and assimilate visual details differently.

Judging the age of babies and young children in photographs presents the least problems as the height, build and general physical appearance of minors offers a better indication of their age than those of fully grown adults. Children's clothing styles in a photograph may also help to define their age group, as explained earlier in the book. When infants and older children appear in a photograph, their ages can usually be assessed accurately to within around two or three years (less with babies) and so once a general time frame for the picture has been determined, it is possible to calculate their earliest and latest probable birth years – dates that can be checked against the family tree. Where several children are present, this information can aid firm identification of a whole family.

Estimating the age of adults in photographs is more difficult. Casual outdoor snapshots depicting family members in everyday situations are more likely to present a natural, realistic impression of their appearance than the professional studio photographs that were expected to provide an attractive, superior portrait: compare, for example, Figs 57 and 131, taken just a few years apart. Also, remember that sometimes appearances can be misleading: we might reasonably assume that our hard-working or disadvantaged ancestors would have physically aged more rapidly than we do today and might therefore look comparatively older in photographs; this may have been the case in reality, but it is not always apparent in formal portraits, especially if the photographer has helpfully retouched the image to flatter his or her subject. In addition, while most of our female forebears would not have used cosmetics to enhance their appearance to a significant degree until at least the 1920s, it was relatively common in the nineteenth century for older men and, especially, women to dye their hair when it began to turn grey, or to don a wig if hair was thinning: some Victorian matrons quite clearly wore wigs that convey the impression of a head of healthy, richly coloured tresses in photographs. Retaining a trim figure, wearing good, well-fitting clothes and paying attention to posture also enhanced our ancestors' over all appearance as they advanced in years (Fig. 78).

If judging an ancestor's likely age from their facial features and any other personal characteristics seems daunting, it may help to focus on their hair and headgear, since in these respects most of our forebears conformed to the general conventions of their time. Youths and young men aged in their early twenties generally appear completely clean-shaven in photographs spanning the entire period covered by this book, while a moustache and/or a beard signified the mature Victorian and Edwardian male: essentially, more facial hair was generally retained for longer by elderly men. Ladies' headwear is also a useful indicator of approximate age and, in earlier photographs, of marital status. In photographs dating from the 1840s and 1850s, a modest day cap or narrow head-covering is invariably worn by married women, as seen in Figs 2 and 82, elderly wives generally favouring the most ornate headwear; however, during the 1860s, the traditional cap grew outmoded among younger wives and from then onwards the trend was for young female ancestors (even if married) to be portrayed bareheaded, or otherwise wearing a fashionable outdoor hat. By contrast, many middle-aged and elderly ladies retained the matronly indoor cap until at least the 1880s, as seen in Fig. 31; evidently some older *un*married ladies wore day caps, too, so in many Victorian images and even some Edwardian photographs, older female ancestors may be wearing ornate lace or frilled caps, whether they were married, widowed or unmarried: essentially the respectable cap that once signified marital status shifted to express age and, perhaps, conservative tastes. Similarly, we notice how many ladies aged in around their forties or fifties and upwards wear black garments that were not mourning attire, but simply expressed the sober, sedate image that society expected of them (Figs 31, 78 and 82). The further away from our own time the photograph, the more clearly age is likely to be expressed in dress and general appearance.

## Judging Likeness and Identity in Family Photographs

Like estimating ancestors' ages, and for many of the same reasons, judging similarity or likeness between the subjects of photographs can be challenging, but all picture researchers attempt this at some stage. We may have to decide whether the same person appears in two or more different images, or whether we are perhaps viewing siblings or cousins who looked alike, or even ancestors of quite different ages who had inherited the same characteristics. Obviously, ascertaining that essential date range for each photograph will determine the correct generation for each subject, which should help to narrow the possibilities, but this may not provide definitive answers. As we know even from modern photographs, confusingly the same person may present quite a different appearance in different images, especially when we compare a professional studio portrait with a casual snapshot; similarly, different people may resemble one another more in some photographs than in others.

When photographs were taken far apart in time, resemblance can be especially hard to gauge. Accurately spotting similarities between images of babies and those of adults is virtually impossible, although adults photographed at different stages of life may have retained their basic facial characteristics and may be possible to identify. To some of us it might seem

**87. *Carte de visite, c.* 1890–2.** This relative was a domestic servant who was photographed at least seven times between 1890 and 1897, when she was young and evidently enjoyed posing for fashionable portraits.

**88. Amateur snapshot, mid-1950s.** It can be hard judging likeness and positively identifying family members in different images, especially when taken far apart in time. This lady, aged in her eighties, is the same relative pictured in Fig. 87, snapped here over sixty years later.

quite obvious that the same ancestor is portrayed in Figs 87 and 88, taken over sixty years apart, in the early 1890s and mid-1950s, respectively, while others may struggle to see a firm likeness, even allowing for the passage of time. Judging facial resemblance is a highly subjective issue: as humans we all have a natural ability to recognise and distinguish between different faces but levels of observation vary from person to person. While an ancestor's prominent facial feature such as a cleft chin or the V-shaped hairline known as a 'widow's peak' might stand out in everyone's eyes, when no such distinguishing mark is present one viewer may be struck by certain aspects of a person's appearance, while another notices different characteristics. There is no easy solution to this dilemma, but families often like to confer over old photographs and where resemblance or identity is in question, perhaps a consensus needs to be reached between as many different viewers as possible.

It also pays to take full advantage of the benefits of modern technology. Scanning equipment and a good image editing programme are especially useful for enhancing old photographs so that they can be studied carefully. Photographs that are inherently murky, like tintypes, or that have become darkened over time can be lightened and brightened, while prints that are marked, scratched or spotted with mildew can be cleaned up to produce a much clearer image. Even improving the resolution of digitised family photographs can make a remarkable difference: simply re-scanning at, say, 600 dpi (dots per inch) and increasing the size of the picture can help significantly when comparing images and studying small details. If researchers are unable to scan or enhance images themselves, there are numerous commercial companies that provide this kind of professional service: look online or in advertisements in the family history magazines.

*Part Three*

# PICTURING PAST LIVES

# Chapter 10

# FAMILY WEDDING PHOTOGRAPHS

Marriage, a common theme of portraiture for centuries, was expressed in the earliest photographic images and remained one of the most popular occasions to be pictured in photographs. Here we consider the special significance of wedding photographs to the family historian, explain how to recognise early marriage scenes and highlight the distinguishing features of wedding photographs from different eras. Family wedding photographs reflect changing social customs and bridal traditions: dress is especially significant, since bridal fashions and the outfits worn by stylish attendants and guests may offer the best method of dating, and ultimately identifying, unfamiliar wedding scenes. We also touch upon newspaper wedding reports as printed descriptions can enhance the pictorial details seen in photographs. The photographic sequence below illustrates a selection of wedding photographs from the 1860s to the 1940s, but many other examples may be viewed online or in books, as listed in the Sources section.

## Special Images

All family historians are familiar with using the national marriage indexes to discover details of ancestors' marriages and record them on the family tree. Wedding photographs add a more tangible dimension to this key aspect of genealogical research, for when a photograph can be linked firmly to a marriage record, that image provides a clear visual expression of the documented fact. Family wedding photographs depict ancestors and more recent relatives from all social backgrounds, can span many decades and may be set in various locations, so as a photographic genre they are extraordinarily varied and full of fascinating historical and social detail. Larger wedding group pictures demonstrate how marriage celebrations drew together diverse relatives for the occasion and, helpfully, they often depict many faces from the past all in the one scene. Wedding pictures are sentimental images that often inspire profound personal attachments and emotions. Conventional poses and fixed facial expressions give little away, yet wedding photographs represent the most powerful of human feelings, recognised throughout time. They also conceal the real-life family dramas that were frequently played out around these occasions and that are often regaled in stories passed down the generations.

## Identifying 'Mystery' Marriages

Inherited wedding photographs generally occupy a treasured position in the family picture collection, and are sometimes carefully documented, or can be easily recognised. Yet some wedding photographs have survived unlabelled and are now unfamiliar to today's researchers. There may be confusion over whose marriages they represent, especially if an ancestor or relative married more than once, or if several weddings occurred in a family within a short period of time. When trying to discover more about 'mystery' wedding photographs, as always, the first step is to establish an accurate date range for the scene. Once a firm time frame has been determined, in many cases it is then possible to link the photograph to a recorded marriage within the family, but if a connection is still proving difficult to make, perhaps the search should be expanded to include the weddings of more distant relatives. We should also

**89. Wedding** *carte de visite*, **1868.** The extravagant 'white wedding' was not firmly established during the nineteenth century. These affluent ancestors wore a luxurious version of regular day clothes for their marriage portrait in 1868.

124

consider the possibility that a wedding photograph preserved by an ancestor or relative may not depict a family wedding at all, but perhaps that of neighbours or friends, which they attended as a guest.

## Recognising Wedding Photographs

Many family historians possess – or have access to – several old wedding photographs, but the number of marriage scenes in the family collection may be even greater than initially realised. It is very easy to overlook a Victorian wedding picture, even when the identities of the subjects are known, because many studio wedding portraits do not display a white bridal gown, flowers, bridesmaids or any of the other attributes that we tend to associate with weddings, as demonstrated by Figs 77 and 89. Positively identifying wedding photographs from among a mass of studio portraits depicting fashionably dressed subjects becomes easier once we understand more about pictorial conventions and past wedding customs.

Following established artistic tradition, many of the first wedding photographs portray the newly-weds posing separately in companion portraits that would later be displayed side by side in the family home: this was common with daguerreotype and ambrotype wedding photographs of the 1840s and 1850s, while later Victorian card-mounted *cartes de visite* and cabinet prints may also occasionally follow this earlier convention. The introduction of the *carte de visite* in 1859/60 brought photography to the masses and photographic evidence indicates that by the mid-1860s newly-weds from various social backgrounds were beginning to mark their special day with a photograph. Since only wealthier Victorian families could afford to hire a professional photographer to attend the actual wedding, if a couple wanted a photograph usually they visited their local studio soon after the ceremony. Special white bridal attire was a novelty and a luxury, an outfit that could not be re-worn, so in most nineteenth-century marriage photographs the couple are wearing their best, most fashionable clothing: generally no special setting was used to suggest the occasion, simply a regular studio set with furniture typical of the era. Usually, the bride and groom posed together, standing or sitting side by side or one was seated, the other standing (Figs 77 and 89). Often the bride's wedding ring was prominently displayed in a marriage photograph and this provides an important identifying clue; however, sometimes it is hard to discern a narrow wedding band, especially if the hand is small, the image faded or damaged. Some poorer couples borrowed a ring for the marriage ceremony, returning it to the lender afterwards, and few men wore a wedding ring until at least the mid-twentieth century. Ultimately, clear signs of marriage are not always evident in Victorian wedding photographs, but we can at least try to identify those images in the collection that are likely to represent the occasion.

## The 'White' Wedding

The 'traditional' white gown and veil popularly associated with brides and weddings developed slowly, over time. Special white bridal wear only became firmly fashionable following the marriage of the young Queen Victoria to Prince Albert of Saxe-Coburg in 1840. Rejecting the heavy state robes worn for earlier royal marriages, the Queen chose a creamy white silk gown with a deep lace flounce – a light ensemble that echoed contemporary evening dress; on her head she wore a circlet of orange blossom with a lace veil, her outfit completed by a long floral-sprigged satin train. Ornamental white bridal dresses with veils were worn again by the Queen's children on their wedding days, grand occasions well publicised in photographs during the late 1850s and 1860s. Thus, under royal influence from the mid-nineteenth century onwards, a frothy white bridal gown and veil became de rigueur for upper and upper middle class weddings: promoted in fashion publications and expressing contemporary notions of innocence and purity, this was the ideal to which all brides aspired, even if unattainable in reality. Alongside this fashion trend, all the familiar trappings of the formal 'white' wedding also came together, including floral decorations, elaborate white cakes and extravagant wedding breakfasts. Formal white weddings were costly affairs: embraced by some of our wealthier Victorian ancestors, for many years they remained beyond the means of most ordinary families.

Generally, the bride's family met the expense of a wedding and although respectable families did their best to rise to the occasion, few working class Victorian fathers could provide their daughters with an elaborate, impractical outfit just for the one day, elegant gowns for bridesmaids and all the other accoutrements of a 'white' wedding. For brides from modest backgrounds the most practical choice was a fashionable coloured day dress, perhaps a new purchase or simply a best gown that could be worn again. As the nineteenth century advanced, more festive elements crept into weddings and the full complement of bridal wear, flowers and bridesmaids became more popular among the middle classes, yet it was not until the early twentieth century that 'white' weddings became more common throughout society. The extraordinary variety of bridal styles adopted by ancestors from different social and occupational backgrounds is evidenced in the diverse array of wedding photographs surviving today, depicting families gathered in settings ranging from photographer's studios and churchyards to vegetable allotments and narrow back yards. By looking more closely at how weddings were pictured at different times and at changing bridal fashions we understand more about our own family wedding photographs and the special occasions that they represent.

## Victorian Wedding Photographs

The earliest known photograph of a bride wearing formal white wedding attire is a Boston daguerreotype taken in 1854, while the first bridesmaids to appear in a photograph relate to the marriage of Princess Victoria to Crown Prince Frederick in 1858; therefore, family historians are highly unlikely to come across photographic representations of these features until significantly later. By the later 1860s elegant outdoor scenes depicting elite weddings may occur in families with affluent ancestry: these images represent elaborately dressed bridal party and guests gathered in the grounds of a substantial villa or country house, taken by a photographer employed for the occasion. At prosperous weddings of this type, the bride and adult bridesmaids wear white silk or muslin dresses with orange-blossom wreaths and lace or tulle veils, their gowns following the prevailing style. Meanwhile, the bride's father, the groom, his best man and groomsmen wear dark frock coats or stylish morning coats with top hats – formal male wedding attire that continued into the 1870s.

Simpler wedding photographs of the period portraying only the bridal couple in the studio generally depict the bride wearing a fashionable coloured daytime outfit made of silk, or the finest affordable fabric. Early–mid-1860s images display the usual wide crinoline skirt, while later in the decade the skirt fullness shifts to the back and by the late 1860s layered garments are evolving

**90. Wedding scene, 1889.** Outdoor wedding group scenes became more common in the later nineteenth century, but even middle-class ancestors often wore fashionable daywear. Here everyone's garment styles and tall hats are typical of the late 1880s.

to accommodate the developing bustle (Fig. 89). Brides' dresses of the early 1870s are always draped over a bustle projection, while after the mid-1870s, following the new elongated cuirass line, bridal garments became narrower and often appear as slender trained 'princess' dresses. Ancestors' wedding gowns have sometimes been carefully preserved within the family and handed down the generations: echoing wedding costumes in museum collections, these heirlooms demonstrate the colours that were fashionable, from the vibrant violets and magentas of the 1860s (following the development of the first synthetic dyes), to the rich russets and browns of the 1870s and 1880s, while black, grey or mauve were usually worn by brides in mourning at the time of their marriage. Depending on their occupation and how they perceived their social status, grooms wore a smart frock coat or the regular three-piece lounge suit that was usual for working class weddings.

As in earlier decades, most family wedding pictures of the 1880s portray a respectably dressed couple in the photographer's studio, for large group photographs set outside were still largely the preserve of middle-class and prosperous ancestors at this time, as seen in Fig. 90. Since bridal outfits followed the prevailing fashion, early in the decade the cuirass line presented a narrow, sheath-like silhouette, skirts typically formed of tiers and sections of kilt-pleating. From around 1884 the revived bustle entered wedding fashions, projecting skirts, tight bodices with ultra-narrow sleeves and tall hats all helping to date wedding photographs of the mid–late 1880s. Many brides, even from comfortably situated families, still wore fashionable coloured daywear at that time, although we notice the trend towards floral accessories, perhaps a floral bodice corsage or a neat bouquet. For grooms and male members of the party, the regular lounge suit continued to serve the working classes, although the stylish morning coat with sloping front edges was popular for more formal weddings, worn with a bowler hat and a white tie, as seen in Fig. 90.

The 1890s saw a rise in the number of larger group wedding scenes – not only those representing high-society marriages but also of the expanding middle classes. Modest studio portraits marking humbler weddings may portray only bride and groom, but more ambitious indoor photographs were beginning to picture wedding parties comprising several people. Additionally, more wedding photographs were being taken outside, reflecting a general growth in outdoor photography at that time and establishing a pattern for future wedding photography (Fig. 91). These images offer a more realistic impression of ancestors' weddings: in particular they show the location where the reception following the church ceremony was held. Wedding scenes of the 1890s also demonstrate the continuing popularity of formal daywear among ordinary and middle-class brides. By mid-decade photographs display vast

**91. Wedding scene, *c.* 1895–6.** The dress worn by bridal parties and wedding guests closely followed fashion, as we see here from the vast 'leg-o'-mutton' sleeves of the mid-1890s. Note how some brides teamed a smart coloured dress with a bridal veil at this time.

puffed 'leg-o'-mutton' sleeves, a taste for elaborate lace panels and frills on bodices and striking headwear, hat brims growing ever wider and crowns piled high with flowers, ribbons, bows and feathers (Fig. 91). The custom for both bride and bridesmaids to wear floral corsages and, sometimes, to carry bouquets was growing, as was the popularity of bridal veils. Therefore, family wedding photographs from the 1890s onwards may be more easily recognisable, even if the bride is wearing a coloured dress. Grooms and male attendants from the lower classes generally wore their 'Sunday best' lounge suit, while gentlemen favoured either the formal black frock coat or morning coat, with plain or striped grey trousers. A white knotted tie or bow tie – the 'correct' wear with evening dress – was also customary for weddings.

**92. Studio group wedding photograph, 1908.** During the early twentieth century gradually more brides throughout society adopted white wedding attire. This Edwardian bride wears a veil, while her bridesmaids wear fashionable hats. The men sport the usual lounge suits and formal white ties.

## Twentieth-century Wedding Photographs

Outdoor group photographs gradually became more common during the early twentieth century and consequently a significant number of Edwardian and later wedding photographs are set outside. Outdoor locations offered more scope to the professional (or amateur) photographer to take several different photographs of the bridal party and guests, so we may begin to notice the survival of more than one depiction of each wedding. Meanwhile, some weddings of the new century recorded in a studio photograph portray either the couple or several figures representing the main bridal party.

Large group photographs often lend Edwardian weddings a sense of grandeur, even though many were relatively low-key affairs. An appearance of luxury was conveyed by the exuberant style of Edwardian women's clothing and accessories, especially the vast hats of the era and the growing vogue for extravagant bridal and bridesmaids' bouquets with trailing greenery (Fig. 92). Fashion favoured pastel shades and lightweight materials like chiffon

**93. Studio wedding portrait, 1919.** A simple studio portrait was always more economical than professional outdoor wedding photographs. Taken just after the First World War, this image shows the vogue for fashionable white wedding garments by the 1910s, worn here with a veil.

and lace, well suited to weddings, although bridal styles varied widely during the early 1900s. In some photographs a special 'white' (cream or ivory) bridal dress is worn, the bodice displaying the high Edwardian neckline and narrow or full sleeves, according to the season's fashions, the gown often worn with a veil, secured with a floral wreath (Fig. 92). However, it was equally common for ordinary brides to wear either a veil or a stylish hat with a fashionable coloured dress or, alternatively, a white hat teamed with a smart white blouse and skirt, expressing the growing vogue for white attire. Adult bridesmaids were often present and were dressed alike, or in different coloured dresses that complemented the bride's outfit, while young flower girls were also fashionable. Late-Victorian conventions surrounding male wedding attire continued into the early 1900s.

During and soon after the First World War studio portraits were common, as seen in Figs 93, 127 and 128, although some 1910s wedding photographs are outdoor scenes: these may be amateur snapshots, reflecting the rise of home photography, while others were clearly taken by a professional photographer. Bridal flowers and bridesmaids continued to feature more widely in weddings, as seen in larger group photographs, the social status of a family possible to gauge from the size of the party, the location or setting, the elegance of the participants and the scale of the floral arrangements. Early in the decade, we notice the sleeker lines of pre-First World War female fashion, whether the bride is wearing either special bridal attire or formal daywear: stylish dresses were in vogue before the war, but by mid-decade fashion favoured more functional suits or blouses and skirts, often tailored in white fabric. Following wider trends, wedding dresses and skirts were worn wider and shorter from around 1915 onwards, the display of the lower leg inspiring the vogue for white stockings and dainty white shoes, especially for summer weddings (Fig. 93). Fashionable headwear usually comprised a wide-brimmed hat with a plain band and subtle decoration (Figs 127 and 128). Until the war, established convention prevailed for men, although a modern knotted tie in a plain colour was beginning to replace the traditional late-Victorian and Edwardian white neck wear. However, during and immediately after the war it was customary for grooms from all social backgrounds serving with the armed forces to wear military uniform on their wedding day, as seen in Chapter 12.

Post-war wedding photographs include the occasional studio portrait, but the preference for outdoor scenes was well established. There were two important royal weddings that engaged the general public in the early 1920s – the marriage of King George V and Queen Mary's daughter, Princess Mary, to Viscount Lascelles in 1922, and that of their second son, Prince Albert, Duke of York, to Lady Elizabeth Bowes-Lyon in 1923. These lavish occasions and the fairytale royal bridal gowns of ivory and silver inspired a new generation of brides and revived the sense of romance that had been largely absent from

**94. Outdoor wedding photograph, 1923.** A white or pale-coloured bridal dress and net veil were popular during the 1920s, reviving the sense of romance that had evaporated during the war. Dress hemlines were long until 1925/6 and headdresses were worn low over the forehead.

wartime weddings. Many 1920s brides chose cream or ivory or fashionable pastel shades such as soft blue, blush pink or lilac, the finest surviving wedding dresses being made of silk and chiffon and embellished with embroidery, lace, pearls and beading. Most 1920s bridal and bridesmaids' dresses were made in afternoon length and since fashionable hemlines fell and rose again throughout the decade, bridal wear followed these shifts, set at mid to low-calf length in the early 1920s (Fig. 94), until around 1926, when they rose dramatically to just below the knee. The fluctuating hemlines of the 1920s and 1930s offer a useful guide for closer dating of unknown weddings of the inter-war era.

Bridal dresses were often teamed with net veils, the headdresses worn low over the forehead (Fig. 94). Alternatively, a fashionable hat could be worn by brides and/or bridesmaids, often a wide-brimmed hat until mid-decade when the neat cloche became the most fashionable style. Adult bridesmaids sometimes wore bandeau-like headdresses in the later 1920s, and there was a

**95. Outdoor wedding photograph, 1934.** Wedding photographs set in the churchyard first become significant during the 1930s, offering a dating clue. This bride wears a cocktail-length, softly draped wedding dress typical of early–mid 1930s styles.

significant fashion for young flower girls to wear distinctive wired headdresses like Dutch caps. Upper and middle-class bridegrooms generally favoured a dark morning coat and grey trousers, these remaining de rigeur for formal weddings throughout the twentieth century. Meanwhile, the average groom and male attendants wore smart lounge suits, the trousers generally very short and narrow in the 1920s and featuring sharp creases and turn-ups (Fig. 94). A coloured plain or patterned silk bow tie or a regular knotted tie was usual, while stylish felt homburg and trilby hats eclipsed the traditional bowler.

As before, a few studio portraits characterise wedding pictures of the 1930s, although outdoor photographs are far more common. By now, views of the bride and her father entering the church (Fig. 95) or bridal couples or groups photographed against the backdrop of the church were coming into vogue – a trend that would develop further in the following decades. Wedding gowns were acquiring a new glamour under the influence of Hollywood films: graceful dresses of plain silk, satin or artificial silk (rayon) fabric sometimes incorporated panels or trimmings of silver lame and were expertly bias-cut to achieve the soft, clinging drape demanded by fashion. They could either be day length (calf length), cocktail length (Fig. 95) or evening length, sweeping the floor, with a long train. Carnations and roses remained popular for bouquets but white lilies became especially fashionable – simple, sophisticated blooms that complemented elegant bridal wear. Bridal styles were diverse during the 1930s and it can be hard to date wedding photographs from this decade very accurately. For example, there was a vogue for summery 'garden party' dresses in flower-print georgette, chiffon or rayon fabrics, which often

**96. Outdoor wedding photograph, North London, 1946.** Although the war was over by the time of this wedding, clothing was still rationed and we can see the influence of Utility styles in the bride's gown and her attendants' dresses. Notice the bridesmaids' short veils, a distinctive 1940s fashion.

had a matching jacket or 'coatee': these were teamed with wide-brimmed hats. However, by the late 1930s, long trained gowns in a pure, bright white satin had largely replaced the earlier soft ivories and creams and such wedding dresses were purposely 'special' garments, not intended to be worn again. Bridesmaids generally wore pastel-coloured plain or floral-sprigged dresses. Grooms from the middle and upper classes favoured a formal morning coat and gentlemanly accessories including silk cravat and top hat, while the average working bridegroom wore a lounge suit tailored in the wide style of the 1930s, his jacket typically double-breasted and featuring sharp lapels.

Despite the Second World War, church wedding ceremonies continued more or less as usual throughout the 1940s and during this decade many more photographs came to be taken in the church doorway, occasionally inside the church. Wartime and post-war bridal gowns and bridesmaids' dresses exhibited their own distinctive style, generally featuring fashionable padded shoulders and either puffed or tight-fitting sleeves, while details like rounded collars or ruched bodices added extra interest (Fig. 96). Cloth shortages dictated that new wedding gowns were made with narrow or slightly flared skirts without trains, but veils were often long and were generally worn well back on the head with tiara-style or tall framed headdresses. Bridesmaids also wore short veils – a helpful 1940s dating clue. However, during and immediately after the war, smart tailored daytime dresses and suits were a common choice (Fig. 139): for more on wartime bridal fashions and photographs see Chapter 12. For grooms not in uniform, the generously cut three-piece lounge suit fashionable before the war was the usual style (Fig. 96).

## Newspaper Wedding Reports

Old newspapers, an important primary source of historical information, may contain specific references to ancestors and relatives and wedding reports exemplify perfectly how notices in the local or national press can complement family photographs. Newspaper wedding reports may provide many more details than surviving Victorian or twentieth-century photographs can suggest, such as the names of the participating families and guests, details of the church ceremony and of the reception, descriptions of the colours and fabrics of the clothing worn, lists of the wedding gifts and other aspects of the occasion. Initially, newspaper reports focused mainly on the society weddings that were of general local or wider national interest, but by the 1880s and 1890s some ordinary weddings were being reported in the press. Sometimes head and shoulders portraits of the bride and groom might be included in reports from the late nineteenth century onwards; after the Second World War almost every British regional newspaper began to publicise news of local weddings, showing photographs of the bride and groom in their wedding attire.

# Chapter 11

# HOME, WORK AND LEISURE

While many surviving photographs of ancestors and relatives can be linked to special occasions such as important rites of passage or wedding celebrations, others reveal a more personal side of their lives – images recording their everyday experiences and activities. Whether outdoor scenes or formal studio portraits, photographs can be of tremendous interest when it comes to discovering more about where and how family members lived, what line of work they pursued and how they spent their leisure time.

## Home Sweet Home
Photographs taken away from the studio in real locations provide an authentic visual record of the past and never more so than when they portray earlier generations in their own familiar surroundings. As we saw in Chapter 4, Victorian or Edwardian photographers sometimes photographed clients at

**97. Freckenham Vicarage (or Rectory), Suffolk, early–mid 1860s.** This early amateur snapshot depicts an affluent family playing the fashionable game of croquet in the back garden of Freckenham Vicarage/Rectory. A rare scene, this offers a wonderful glimpse of upper class mid-Victorian domestic life.

home (see Figs 37 and 80), while snapshots of family members standing on their doorstep, front path, in the street outside the house, or in their back garden were even more popular themes of amateur photography (Figs 39, 49, 56, 58, 85, 88 and 97–100). Throughout the period covered by this book the vast majority of domestic scenes were set outdoors, since taking photographs required a good source of light. The sunny glass conservatory of a spacious Victorian villa could work (Fig. 68), but, as explained in Chapter 1, interior views of the average family house are uncommon until at least the mid-twentieth century.

Photographs set in the vicinity of the family home sometimes depict their subject(s) in an unidentifiable garden, although more often they include all, or part, of a house, cottage, or an outbuilding such as a garage, barn or stables, along with a portion of garden or grounds. Such images occur in most family photograph collections and it may be possible to identify their location if, for example, they represent relatives' homes remembered from the past, perhaps from childhood visits, or if older family members recognise the scene. Some of the properties pictured in photographs will have been occupied for many years and may still be a family home today. Far from being simply bricks and mortar, home was fundamental to forebears' everyday lives – the setting for many of the events and experiences that make up human existence and shape family life. In some cases a home may have been combined with business premises, domestic routine and occupational operations being conducted under one roof, as in the case of the public house depicted in Fig. 142. Where sequential photographs of the same property survive, taken at different dates, these provide an interesting visual history of the house and its development over time, demonstrating the maturing or re-landscaping of the garden, building extensions and structural renovations, reflecting the changing lives, needs and tastes of the occupants.

Naturally, the family properties seen in old photographs can vary widely in size, type and architectural style, depending on the geographical location and forebears' social status. The elegant townhouses or country estates of prosperous Victorian ancestors may sometimes appear in professional photographs, for example elite wedding scenes. Nineteenth-century amateur snapshots are rare, but when they do occur, they too are likely to connect to affluent ancestors with substantial residences, as seen in Fig. 97, a genteel croquet scene in the picturesque garden of an eighteenth-century Suffolk vicarage. Country houses and other buildings of particular historical or architectural interest occurring in family photographs may have survived into the twenty-first century; if so, they are possibly listed buildings, so it is worth consulting the British Listed Buildings website for more information: www.britishlistedbuildings.co.uk. Remember that a manor house, estate farmhouse, rectory, mill house or other significant residence – and its

**98. Unidentified garden scene,** *c.* **1901–5.** Amateur photography was still relatively uncommon at the beginning of the 1900s, but Edwardian snapshots occur in some collections and often portray the middle and upper classes enjoying leisure time at home with friends and relatives.

occupants – will have been well known in the neighbourhood, so it may also be helpful to conduct research using sources for the relevant geographical area, to see what local information is available. See Chapter 13 for more on local history research.

Nineteenth and early twentieth-century photographs may show the kind of handsome brick villas with spacious grounds that typify the homes of middle-class ancestors (Fig. 98). However, more common are images of the modest Victorian or Edwardian terraced or semi-detached houses that had sometimes been built for workers and their families: see, for example, Figs 91, 99 and 123. Some of our past family members occupied such properties throughout their lives, as tenants or owners, although between the wars and again after the Second World War many city dwellers vacated ageing buildings

**99. At home at North Warnborough, Hampshire, late 1920s.** By the inter-war era many families had acquired their own cameras and took photographs of everyday scenes, as well as special occasions. This boy, posing outside the family house, is smartly dressed and may have been about to go to school.

**100. At home at Victor Villas, Lower Edmonton, North London, 1944.** Many family snapshots depict ancestors and relatives posing outside their homes. This family moved from their Victorian house in Islington to a modern property in the developing suburbs during the 1930s.

that had no integral bathroom or electricity and moved into new homes with modern conveniences, perhaps urban blocks of flats or houses in the burgeoning suburbs. Many families bought their first property during and following the house-building boom of the 1920s and 1930s and consequently in family photographs we often see relatives posing proudly in front of new homes displaying fresh brickwork and newly paved paths (Figs 88 and 100).

Some of the family houses and gardens pictured in photographs may not be instantly recognisable, but where ancestors or relatives in the scene can be identified and when an accurate date range has been determined for the image, census returns can be consulted to establish the address and location. Inevitably, investigating the properties pictured in family photographs as part of the genealogical research process also links closely with house history research, a popular subject about which much is published and for which many helpful documents survive to aid those beginning investigations. Particularly useful are census returns, electoral registers and old directories that listed the head of the household. Maps, plans and land surveys are also invaluable when trying to locate an ancestral home, especially as a house name, street number or even the road may have changed over the years. If the precise address of a former family residence can be determined and its location found, it can be rewarding to pay a personal visit, taking along old photographs to compare with the present-day property. If the current occupants are at home and available to chat, it may be that they know something of the house's history and can add to the family details already recorded. For some genealogists, pursuing the family house trail is all part of the fun of tracing their roots, but if conducting this kind of research isn't possible, there are reliable professional organisations whose skilled 'house detectives' can provide this service: look online for house historians, or consult advertisements in relevant publications.

## Working Lives

Some photographs of ancestors or relatives inform us about their working lives, whether consciously or incidentally. These images may be professional studio portraits, semi-formal photographs taken with other work colleagues at their place of work or casual snapshots of family members carrying out their daily tasks, 'off duty' but dressed for work.

As we saw in Chapter 6, career achievement often resulted in a special commemorative portrait: this might be inspired by completion of a training course, initial entry into work, the start of a new job or attainment of a higher professional grade or rank. Sometimes the occupational context is not clear from the photograph, especially if the subject is wearing everyday garments: however, a significant number of our forebears wore a regulated form of dress for work that identified and defined their role, and this uniform would be proudly modelled in the picture, as seen in Figs 101 and 102. Amateur snapshots taken using a personal camera may also portray past family members wearing an occupational uniform, either while engaged in work, as seen in Fig. 103, or relaxing after work hours (Fig. 104).

Broadly, work uniforms can be divided into military uniforms and 'civilian' (non-military) uniforms. Army, navy, air force and associated uniforms are discussed further in Chapter 12. The civilian uniforms sometimes seen in

**101. Studio portrait,
c. 1902–10.** Identifying the civilian uniform worn by this Southampton dock worker required the expertise of four dress/uniform experts before it was recognised as that of the short-lived International Mercantile Marine Company, a shipping line established in 1902.

family photographs were chiefly associated with particular occupations, including domestic servants, medical workers, public servants – postal workers and members of the fire brigade and police force – and transport company employees: ship, train, tramways and bus crews. Ancestors and relatives working in service industries may also have worn uniforms, for example, hotel, restaurant and cafe staff, or cinema employees, while many factories and mills also demanded standard work wear that met safety criteria: a uniform of sorts. Attachment to certain organisations also entailed adopting prescribed forms of dress, for example membership of the Salvation Army, whose female members were identified by their sober clothing and old-fashioned bonnets (Fig. 102). Some of the uniforms devised for jobs in the past were ultimately short-lived, while others underwent a series of changes over time and may still exist in modern form today.

Civilian uniforms are fascinating, but can be hard to date and to identify positively when they occur in a family photograph: this was the case with Fig. 101, which was studied by four different dress and uniform experts before the uniform was firmly identified. In general, buttons, cap badges and sometimes sleeve insignia can identify the organisation that employed the

**102. Studio portrait,** *c.* **1904–9.** Female members of the Salvation Army were expected to wear sedate dark garments and modest mid-Victorian-style bonnets, even in the twentieth century: the style of this ancestor's blouse and tailored skirt confirm an Edwardian date.

**103. Amateur snapshot, 1913.** Many of our forebears worked as domestic servants and may have been photographed at work, wearing their uniforms. This nanny wears the typical dark dress, white apron with narrow bib and neat cap of the early 1910s.

wearer and in the case of uniforms with a long history, individual photographs can be broadly dated from details such as helmet and garment styles, since their dates of introduction have usually been recorded. Unfortunately, research still needs to be carried out into this subject: there is no one printed or Internet source covering the development of all kinds of work uniform, although books on the history of occupational dress include those categories of workers who wore civilian uniforms (see Sources). There are also many publications about specific occupations that may feature descriptions and illustrations of past uniforms: search online for useful titles, or consult the catalogues of publishers like Pen & Sword Books, Shire Books and the Society of Genealogists, all of whom produce occupation-related books. In addition, many official organisations and private individuals run special-interest websites and some of these incorporate a uniform section displaying photographs, perhaps even surviving uniforms: some useful online sources are listed at the back of the book.

Many of our ancestors did not wear a regulated form of dress, yet may have been photographed in a studio with the tools of their trade, perhaps to mark completion of an apprenticeship or becoming a Master of their craft or profession. Photographs may also survive of ancestors at work, as seen in Figs 103, 105, 141–5 and 148. It is interesting to view past family members in their working environments, going about their daily tasks, perhaps driving

**104. Amateur snapshot, *c*. 1917–19.** This photograph is only closely dateable from the fashionably dressed ladies. During the 1910s nurses wore modest calf-length dresses protected by a starched apron: their dress colour was often blue, but cap styles varied.

vehicles or using machinery or other equipment: for example, they may have run or assisted with a local business (see Chapter 13), toiled outdoors in the fields or had their duties cut out for them as a domestic servant. Outdoor manual workers tended to wear a practical, hard-wearing version of regular dress, often discarding outer garments for comfort and easier movement (Figs 105, 145 and 148), while bank and office workers ('white-collar' workers) and shop staff were expected to look smart and well groomed (Figs 143(a) & (b)). Today, increasing numbers of vintage work-related photographs are being displayed on the Internet: browsing such images helps with visualising different occupations and may even suggest an approximate date for undated family photographs. A simple Google Images search can reveal some great pictures, while the popular image sharing site Flickr, used by archives, museums and by individuals, is especially recommended. On Flickr there are growing sets of occupational photographs, for example at www.flickr.com/search/?q= occupational+photos.

Finally, if information about a work-related photograph or unidentifiable uniform cannot be found anywhere in a book or online, it may be a good idea to post the image and query on a family history forum or submit them to the

**105. Amateur snapshot, dated 1918**. This snapshot, identified on the reverse and dated 1918, depicts a farming ancestor using horse-drawn machinery at Hinton Woodlands in Hampshire. Such scenes provide a realistic view of our forebears' working lives.

help pages of a genealogy magazine. Alternatively, for a professional opinion, consider consulting a qualified dress historian or photograph specialist, who should be able to date and perhaps also positively identify the scene.

## The Great Outdoors

Although some of our Victorian and Edwardian ancestors were photographing the world around them at an early date, most families did not acquire their first camera until at least the 1910s and it was not until the inter-war era that many households gained a family photographer who would enthusiastically snap all kinds of occasions. Besides domestic scenes, it was also common for amateur photographers to take photographs of day trips, weekend excursions and holidays. From the 1920s onwards, as the division between work and leisure time became more pronounced and fresh air and physical exercise came to be better appreciated, more of our family members began to get out and about regularly as a form of relaxation, to enjoy the countryside, seaside and to visit other areas of the country. This growing trend is reflected in the nature of the photographs that survive in family collections recording the outings and holidays taken by more recent generations.

Walking, hiking and rambling all became popular activities during the

**106. Amateur snapshot, dated 1938.** Inter-war snapshots reveal the popularity of cycling as a sporting and leisure activity. Pictured on an Easter tour of Wales, the relative on the left wears a modern zip-up bomber jacket with plus fours; his friends wear casual jerseys, open-necked shirts and shorts.

1920s and 1930s, walkers often taking a train out of the city then exploring the local countryside on foot. Cycling, enjoyed by enthusiasts since the 1880s, also became hugely popular as the design and functioning of bicycles steadily improved and machines became more affordable: from the 1920s onwards and especially during the 1930s many family snapshots depict relatives with their bicycles, even tandems. This was the heyday of the bicycle, when cycling was still a safe and pleasurable pastime, before large numbers of motor vehicles took over the roads: cycling was a common mode of everyday transport, while groups of young friends and members of cycling clubs enjoyed outings and cycling holidays (Fig. 106).

**107. Postcard photograph, early–mid-1920s.** Between the wars, when relatively few households owned cars, many people enjoyed charabanc outings to the countryside or coast, with relatives, friends, work colleagues or members of a social club or group: they often posed for a souvenir photograph.

Touring by motor car also became fashionable during the 1920s and 1930s, mainly among the affluent upper and middle classes (Fig. 39), but for those without vehicles, motor charabancs were a popular form of transportation to beauty spots and other places of interest. Sometimes individuals or family groups might book a ride from charabanc company touts at the beach or on the street, but often a charabanc outing would be organised by a local company for its workers, by a public house for its 'regulars' or by a social club for its members (Fig. 107). During the 1920s and 1930s charabancs were a familiar sight throughout the British countryside, but eventually they declined with the increase in private-car ownership. Many of our forebears learned to drive vehicles during the Second World War, encouraging a dramatic rise in private motor-car sales; consequently, snapshot photographs from the 1940s onwards reveal more ordinary working families beginning to enjoy the freedom and mobility afforded by their own cars – trips to the coast, country picnics, family outings and journeys to visit friends and relatives (Fig. 108).

One of the factors that encouraged increasing enjoyment of the outdoors after the First World War was a major shift in social attitudes towards open-air activity and sun exposure: whereas sunburnt skin and freckles had once been the unwelcome sign of outdoor manual labour and were avoided at all costs by the genteel classes, during the 1920s acquiring a suntan began to symbolise the reverse – money and leisure time. Originating in the glamorous resorts of the French Riviera and California, sunbathing for its own sake and developing a glowing sun tan rapidly became fashionable elsewhere and by the end of the decade holidaymakers on British beaches were stripping off layers of concealing clothing and exposing more of their bodies. Rapidly swimwear design advanced from this time onwards, women's bathing costumes becoming more cut away and revealing, although many men and boys retained the traditional vest section to their costumes throughout the 1930s (Fig. 109). Photographs can be dated from styles of beachwear and other holiday and leisure clothes, just as they can be dated from more formal clothing: by the 1930s and 1940s, we notice more casual, comfortable forms of dress and lightweight sportswear being worn in photographs, such as sleeveless sundresses for women (Fig. 39) and shorts for men (Fig. 106) – modest garments to our modern eyes, but innovative seventy or eighty years ago and a clear indication of changing times.

**108. Amateur snapshot, 1940s.** Picnics in the countryside had always been popular occasions, but day excursions became much easier once families acquired their own motor cars. The dresses and hairstyles of the young women date this unidentified scene to the 1940s.

**109. Holiday snapshot, 1935.** Before cheap package trips abroad became available, many families enjoyed summer holidays in Britain. Annotated 'Worthing, August 1935', this snapshot demonstrates the new vogue for acquiring a suntan and skimpier bathing costumes for women.

## Sporting Pursuits

Many of our ancestors and more recent relatives enjoyed sports, either as spectators or participants. During the nineteenth and early twentieth centuries organised sporting events advanced, with rules becoming more standardised and permanent facilities established, for example, for city football clubs and county cricket teams. Local clubs, groups and organisations for activities from cycling to athletics proliferated, increasingly municipal parks provided facilities such as public tennis courts, while many local swimming pools and lidos opened throughout the country, especially during the 1920s and 1930s. Schools – initially public schools, but later state schools – taught team games and PE classes ranging from rugby and hockey to gymnastics as part of the curriculum, sporting prowess also being encouraged at colleges and universities. The progress of sport and a keener interest in health and physical fitness coincided with advances in amateur photography and we may well encounter visual evidence of the sporting interests of past family members among our picture collections.

In the Victorian era few sports were open to women, although genteel ladies enjoyed archery and croquet, while lawn tennis first became fashionable in the mid-1870s. Croquet was a respectable, leisurely pastime enjoyed at home by both men and women, especially from the 1860s onwards, and is often pictured in photographs portraying affluent ancestors in their country gardens, as seen in Fig. 97. Gradually, more sports opened up to both sexes, although for many years certain activities were restricted to or dominated by men and boys. Our male predecessors may well have participated in energetic sports like running, boxing (Fig. 110) and football (Fig. 146), but during the early twentieth century more sedate games requiring skill and judgement became increasingly popular with both men and women, such as golf (Fig. 111) and lawn bowls (Fig. 112).

R.W. Elliott, ALDERSHOT.

**110. Studio portrait,** *c.* **1901–5.** Before amateur photography became commonplace a sporting ancestor might visit the studio to demonstrate his or her hobby. This boy, a keen boxer, wears Edwardian-style athletics or sports vest and drawers with soft pumps.

**111. Amateur snapshot, early 1910s.** Golf became increasingly popular as a middle-class sport during the early twentieth century, attracting both male and female players and onlookers. Golfing dress included breeches or plus fours for men and comfortable woollen suits for women.

Our parents, grandparents or great-grandparents may have trained regularly at a gym or club, possibly becoming proficient in their activity at an early age (Fig. 110), perhaps eventually becoming serious sportsmen or women. Some may have joined a local football or cricket team, or a pony or bowls club, perhaps excelling at competitive events and winning championships against other teams or clubs at county or even national level: if so, official team photographs may well survive, portraying them wearing their sports kit or club uniform (Fig. 146), or posing proudly with medals, badges, cups and trophies (Fig. 112). For more ideas about investigating local sports clubs, see Chapter 13. Amateur snapshots tend to demonstrate the more casual side of sports and may, for example, depict family members riding a new bicycle, practising their golfing technique (Fig. 111) or having a friendly knockabout on the tennis court (Fig. 113).

Sometimes we may already be aware that an ancestor or relative engaged in a certain sport, especially if they played at an advanced level, although,

**112. Studio portrait, 1935.** Family members might visit a professional studio to celebrate a significant sporting triumph. These stylish ladies, wearing blazers, white dresses and hats in their bowls-club colours and posing with trophies, were England Pairs Champions in 1935.

**113. Amateur snapshot, late 1930s.** Tennis, fashionable since the late nineteenth century, became increasingly popular between the wars and tennis scenes often feature among family snapshots. This relative was fortunate to play on a private outdoor court at home.

unlike occupations, often details of leisure interests went unrecorded, so surviving sporting photographs can provide unique evidence of how forebears spent their spare time. Belonging to a sports club could also be a very sociable activity: whole families would watch as their relatives played a match and various social functions such as teas, dinners and dances were centred on the clubhouse. So, involvement in sports and the social activities surrounding membership of a team or club often played a major role in the lives of earlier generations.

# Chapter 12

# WARTIME PHOTOGRAPHS

Many of our family members participated in the First or Second World War and all who lived through the war years would have been profoundly affected by their experiences. Photographs taken during the two major conflicts of the twentieth century reflect the life-changing events of those turbulent times and are among the most treasured pictures to have been handed down the generations. Whether formal portraits set in the commercial photographer's studio, outdoor group scenes or casual family snapshots, these poignant images tell of adventure, fortitude, bravery, camaraderie, love, loss, sacrifice, pain and hope.

**114. Studio portrait of arm[y] chaplain.** Soldiers' spiritual was the concern of the Army Chaplains' Department, who[se] chaplains, or padres, were ra[nk] and dressed as officers. This [one] wears his officer's Sam Brow[ne] and a clerical collar instead o[f a] regular collar and tie.

## First World War: July 1914–November 1918
### First World War Photography
Many families have inherited photographs relating to the First World War. This was the first major conflict in which photography played a significant role at all levels, being used for surveying and mapping territory, for producing propaganda material and also for creating personal mementoes. Those commercial photographers able to continue operating during the war were kept busy taking formal studio portraits in their usual premises or might be hired to come out to photograph semi-formal military or occupational group scenes. Amateur photography was also on the rise during the 1910s as more people acquired their first camera and began to take spontaneous snapshots. Many army officers took cameras away with them to the Western Front to record their experiences, like Field Marshall (Earl) Haig, whose First World War 'official photographs' can be viewed on the National Library of Scotland's Flickr set: www.flickr.com/photos/nlscotland/sets/7215762415 0609895.

154

Despite discouragement from the senior ranks and an official ban on troop photography in 1915, some combatants did photograph the scenes around them when an opportunity arose. However, early box and folding cameras were still relatively unwieldy and personal camera ownership was not yet widespread throughout society, so most photographs of the trenches and battlefields were taken by army officers or by the official war photographers who were first appointed in March 1916. Censorship of visual material during the war reflected government concern that only selected images were published in Britain, uplifting scenes depicting heroism and military success

**115. Studio portrait, *c*. 1914–16.** This young soldier, wearing the standard khaki service dress of the First World War, is identifiable as a Grenadier Guardsman from his cap badge and his three-piece brass shoulder titles. Dressed for 'walking out' after duty, he wears a 1908 pattern webbing belt and carries a swagger stick or cane.

**116. Studio portrait, pre-April 1916.** Older men or those in essential civilian jobs could serve with the Volunteer Training Corps and initially wore a military style uniform in grey-green cloth. The abolition in April 1916 of the distinctive red armband with GR cipher, seen here, helps to date this photograph: later in 1916 a khaki uniform was introduced.

that would boost public morale and encourage men at home to join the war effort. Some disturbing photographs did emerge and images are still being uncovered today, but they were not widely circulated during the conflict and are relatively rare in today's family photograph collections. The majority of snapshots taken by family members during this period are set in Britain and depict civilian life, work scenes, low-key weddings or soldiers at home on leave.

Photographic evidence suggests that the First World War images surviving within most family archives broadly follow certain themes. Examining these in more detail aids our understanding of these photographs taken around a century ago and suggests how they would have fitted in with ancestors' and relatives' experiences of the war.

## The New Recruit

In Chapter 6 we looked at the convention for family members to pose for a formal studio portrait if they had successfully completed a training course or entered a new profession, wearing their occupational uniform if demanded of the position. Needless to say, this type of photographic occasion became common during the First World War as forebears volunteered or were conscripted into the armed forces. Millions of men and women donned uniforms of one description or another that firmly identified their wartime role and responsibilities. New recruits were often inspired to visit their local photography studio, proudly modelling their pristine uniform for a special portrait that signified they were fulfilling their patriotic duty and indicated their status as military or naval personnel or members of support organisations. Many of today's photograph collections include portraits commemorating the successful completion of initial training or a new wartime appointment, whether our ancestor or relative was, for example, an army officer (Fig. 114), a guardsman (Fig. 115), a volunteer (Fig. 116) or a young woman about to join the war effort (Fig. 117). All ranks, regiments, roles and war-related organisations may be represented in this kind of photograph.

## Departure for War

Studio photographs that portray forebears as new recruits may also be signalling their imminent departure, for having undergone basic training, many would have been about to be deployed or had already been given their marching orders and had precious little time in which to organise a photograph. So, as well as celebrating achievement, subjects would have already been looking ahead with anticipation and no doubt trepidation towards an uncertain future – one that appeared increasingly uncertain as the war advanced. Some photographs suggest that family members visited the studio specifically to mark their departure – one last picture on home soil before

**117. Voluntary Aid Detachment recruit, 1918.** This 17-year-old relative, posing in her new nurse's outdoor uniform, had just passed her first-aid and nursing examinations as a Voluntary Aid Detachment recruit and was about to commence medical duties in a military hospital at Freshwater on the Isle of Wight, in 1918.

**118. Family studio photograph.** This farewell photograph of a mature soldier pictured with his wife and three young children demonstrates how men from all walks of life entered the First World War. His 1914-pattern leather belt, typically worn by Infantry Service battalions, was introduced in haste to equip a rapidly expanding army.

leaving family and friends behind. Soldier brothers sometimes posed together in uniform, or a youth might be pictured with one or two friends from the same town, their photographs left with their families as a precious keepsake, while the men might take away with them images of their parents, siblings, sweethearts and wives. A husband and father about to leave for war would typically be photographed with his wife and children in the studio before his departure. Such images are a reminder that, due to manpower shortages, mature men with steady civilian careers and families to support were also drawn into the First World War and were often drafted into one of the many Infantry Service battalions (Fig. 118). A copy of a farewell family scene would be taken away to war, while another might remain at home.

**119. Royal Artillery horseman.** Mounted soldiers wore spurs and a leather ammunition bandolier across their shoulders. This rider's uniform identifies him as a member of the Royal Artillery, one of the army's largest regiments which used horses to draw its guns into action.

Today's surviving images depicting husbands, fathers, brothers and sons, or daughters and sisters, about to embark on wartime duties capture a critical moment in time, portraying our First World War forebears on the brink of new experiences that might either be the making or the death of them. Farewell photographs played a crucial role in maintaining connections, visually at least, between those at home and their relatives away at war. Tragically, some would turn out to be their last ever likeness and they subsequently gained a heightened significance as memorial portraits of the deceased.

## On Service

Sometimes photographs taken throughout the course of the war offer a glimpse of where a past family member was based or what their role entailed. Although the British army had embarked on a programme of mechanisation before the First World War, large sections relied on horse-drawn transport: soldiers with a mounted role, whether photographed in uniform in a

**120. British Red Cross Society ambulance crews with ambulance.** The army's medical services in France and Belgium were augmented by members of the British Red Cross Society who served as ambulance crews in khaki uniform with Red Cross badges and armbands. Their uniforms followed military style, those of the men having buttoned collars, officers wearing collars and ties and cuff rank badges.

**121. Studio portrait, India, c. 1916–18.** This soldier wears the typical lightweight khaki drill uniform with shorts that was reserved for hot climates. The cloth flash on his helmet demonstrates that he was with the 6th Battalion of the Royal Sussex Regiment, who, originally a cyclist battalion, were converted to infantry serving in India in February 1916.

commercial studio or outdoors with their horse, are depicted wearing spurs and the leather ammunition bandolier worn diagonally across their shoulders that was more practical for horsemen than the cumbersome waist belt and pouches worn by infantry men (Fig. 119). Although forebears serving with the forces on the front line are unlikely to feature in any action photographs, they may well appear in a semi-formal group photograph organised by their unit (Fig. 120). This kind of photograph was probably commissioned from local French and Belgian professional photographers and all, or most, of the men in the scene would purchase a copy of the photograph as a personal memento.

The First World War is chiefly remembered for the horrors of trench warfare in Belgium and France and indeed many of our forebears served on the Western Front; consequently, it is sometimes forgotten that British and Empire soldiers also served in other theatres of war, for example, in East Africa against Germany and in the Middle East against Germany's ally Turkey, or may have been stationed as far away as India. Sometimes photographs were taken overseas in foreign studios, indicating where family members were posted with their battalions (Figs 121 and 122(a)). Those serving in hot climates were issued with modified kit that reflected the environment: this included a lightweight khaki drill uniform with shorts and instead of regular caps or steel helmets, the Universal khaki or pith helmet, believed to offer protection from sunstroke. Metal cap badges were not usually worn on tropical headwear, but were replaced by coloured cloth flashes sewn to the khaki binding or *pugaree* wound round the helmet.

## Thinking of You

One kind of photograph associated mainly with the First World War, but that occasionally occurs in other contexts, is the image with the clear but unspoken theme: 'You may be far away, but in my heart you are close by' or 'Thinking of you while we are far apart' – or sentiments to that effect. Figs 122(a) & (b)

**122(a). Studio portrait, Alexandria, Egypt, *c.* 1916–18.** Dressed in khaki drill uniform, a brass coat of arms badge on his cuffs indicating his rank, this Sergeant Major of the North Staffordshire Regiment after serving at Gallipoli would have gone with the 7th (Service) Battalion to Egypt in January 1916. A vignette photograph of his family in the corner shows that they are in his thoughts.

**122(b). Studio portrait, *c.* mid-1910s.** From the same collection as 122(a), this portrait of the soldier's family was either taken to war, or perhaps sent to him while he was away. Demonstrating the popular sentiment 'Thinking of you while we are apart', he had this image inserted into a photograph taken in Egypt that would then have been posted to them at home.

demonstrate how a soldier serving overseas might be photographed in a foreign studio and have a small vignette image deriving from an existing photograph of his sweetheart or family inserted into the corner, to express his constant thoughts of those at home. Posted back to the family or fiancée in question, the recipient(s) who anxiously awaited the serviceman's return would know that they had not been forgotten, despite the distance separating them from their loved one, and the photograph would be treasured as a sentimental emblem.

## At Home

Families eagerly looked forward to their men folk coming home on leave and those who had recently acquired a camera would have enjoyed taking snapshots of the family temporarily reunited, relaxing at home and making the most of their precious time together before the serviceman returned (Fig. 123). In some instances a photograph can be dated from the details of the uniform worn to soon after the end of the war: it was not unusual for a member of the services to have one last photograph taken in uniform around the time of their demobilisation, wearing any medal ribbons that he had been awarded. A young soldier, sailor or airman might pose alone in the studio (Fig. 124), or, if he was married with a family, perhaps in a group scene portraying him happily reunited with his wife and children. Such photographs demonstrated proud completion of war service, an overwhelming sense of relief at having come through safely and the long-anticipated return to family and home.

**123. Amateur snapshot, Norwood, 1916.** Here two sisters pose with their brother at home on leave in this amateur snapshot. His boot spurs and riding crop indicate that this Sergeant rode a horse when on duty, while his cap badge with crossed carbines and Hampshire rose arm badge (worn by Senior NCOs) denote service with the Hampshire Yeomanry (Carabiniers).

**124. Studio portrait, Ramsgate, *c.* 1919.** Some family members served with the Royal Navy, which was active throughout the war. This sailor, whose medal ribbons indicate that he was photographed after the end of the conflict, wears on his left arm the badge of the Minesweeping Service. Sea mines posed a major threat to shipping and were cleared by minesweeping ships.

## Female Photographs

Most First World War military photographs surviving in family collections depict male ancestors and relatives, although the Great War was the first time that uniformed women made a significant contribution to the war effort. All of the armed services recruited females to replace men in non-combatant roles: the Women's Army Auxiliary Corps (WAAC), Women's Royal Naval Service (WRNS) and Women's Royal Air Force (WRAF) (Fig. 125). Family photographs may reveal how young women played an active role during the war, extending their horizons and learning new skills. Many wore distinctive dress that identified their position, whether occupational uniforms as, for example, in the case of nurses (Fig. 117), or military uniforms as recruits into the military units (Fig. 125). Special civilian uniforms were also devised for female transport workers and for Land Army girls who adopted practical knee-length overall-coats, breeches and gaiters.

As manpower shortages during the First World War saw growing numbers

**125. Members of the Women's Royal Air Force, *c.* 1918.** This group from the Women's Royal Air Force pose outside a civilian garage and were probably serving as motor drivers. Their caps and arms carry the winged eagle of the RAF, which was formed in April 1918. The right-hand figure wears the two stripes of a Corporal.

**126. Munitions factory workers, First World War.** These 'munitionettes' wear practical khaki overall coats and caps to secure their hair, while several of them also display the triangular brass 'On War Service' badge issued to those involved in essential government work. By the end of the war nearly 1 million women were employed in munitions production.

of men in civilian employment called up for the services, their place was taken by women. Among the many essential jobs covered by females, a large number served in the government's munitions factories producing ammunition such as gun shells and rifle bullets for the war effort. The 'munitionettes', as they were called, and the thousands of women manning mills and refineries and working in heavy industry all adopted functional work clothes ranging from calf-length overall coats (Fig. 126) to shorter tunics and trousers. Photographs of the capable First World War female worker, wearing a smart calf-length skirt and belted tunic, or sturdy trousers or breeches – masculine garments considered unacceptable before the war – survive in their thousands today, in both public and private family collections. These iconic images demonstrate visibly the enormous impact of war on many of our female forebears' lives.

### First World War Wedding Photographs

As mentioned in Chapter 10, marriage photographs taken during the First World War were often modest studio portraits of the bride and groom (Figs 93, 127 and 128), although outdoor wedding scenes sometimes occur. Many weddings of the period were simple or hurried events, perhaps organised at short notice to pre-empt a serviceman's departure for war, or to coincide with a brief period of leave. Invariably, the groom wore his military uniform for the occasion: a bride might possibly wear special white bridal wear, although more common was a smart daytime suit or dress, accessorised with a stylish hat – an outfit that could be assembled quickly and worn again in the future (Figs 127 and 128). Tragically, a First World War-era wedding portrait may have been the only photograph taken of the couple together if the groom did not survive the war.

**127. Studio wedding photograph, dated September 1917.** The collar and tie, jacket style and leather Sam Browne belt identify this groom as an officer, the two brass shoulder pips indicating his rank of Lieutenant. His cap and collar badges feature a maple leaf, demonstrating that he served with a regiment of the Canadian army. The bride wears a smart civilian suit with fashionable accessories.

**128. Studio wedding photograph,** *c.* **1918.** This groom wears the standard khaki service dress of the First World War, his rank of Corporal indicated by the two chevrons on his sleeves. His cap badge is that of the Northumberland Fusiliers, whose battalions mostly served on the Western Front. The bride wears a fashionable dress and wide-brimmed hat typical of the years 1917–19.

## Second World War: September 1939–May 1945 (in Europe)

Family photographs surviving from the years spanning the Second World War – a more recent event, closer to our own time – are, predictably, more numerous and more varied than those for the First World War. Besides professional studio portraits and formal group photographs, many more amateur snapshots exist for the 1939–45 war than for the earlier conflict. We also notice significant numbers of women in uniform, as well as men, reflecting the even greater role played by females in both military units and support organisations during the Second World War. With a multitude of wartime roles coming into existence, including many connected to home-front duties, we see a wide variety of Second World War uniforms represented in our picture archives.

## Studio Photographs

Just as they were during the First World War, those commercial photography studios still operating in Britain and abroad were occupied throughout the course of the Second World War and in its aftermath. Professional studio

**129. Studio portrait, Second World War naval officer.** Naval officers' rank was indicated by the number of gold braid bars worn on the cuff, this style of twisted braid that of a Sub-Lieutenant in the Royal Naval Reserve. The small silver badge shows that this man served with the Royal Navy Patrol Service: his age and jacket medal ribbons suggest that he may have been a First World War veteran.

photography at this time was generally of a high quality and intimate portraits that paid close attention to lighting and angle of the subject's head and shoulders provide clear facial and dress details and often evoke a sense of 1940s glamour.

Continuing a familiar theme, many Second World War studio portraits in family collections portray both male and female new recruits into the armed forces or other wartime organisations, family members who had perhaps successfully completed their initial training and commissioned a professional photograph displaying the new uniform that they had earned the right to wear. Sometimes photographs reveal how male relatives who had already served in the First World War were going to war for a second time, as experienced veterans (Fig. 129). As the conflict continued, extending over a longer time period than the

**130. Studio portrait, dated November 1942.** Airmen of the RAF wore a collar and tie with their uniform. At the top of this serviceman's sleeve is the usual RAF eagle and below it the two-bladed propellor badge indicating his rank of Leading Aircraftman. The white peak at the front of his blue cap indicates that he is undergoing training to fly as an aircrewman.

**131. Studio portrait, dated October 1944.** This newly promoted Sergeant wears the identifying three stripes on his sleeve, and the small brass grenade partially visible above is unique to Sergeants of the Royal Engineers. The upper cloth badge displaying a triangle demonstrates his role in one of the Airfield Construction Groups who served in Europe after D-Day. The sleeveless leather jerkin was issued for winter.

Great War, many of our relatives in the forces received advanced training and promotion and newly promoted or qualified servicemen and women might often visit a photographer to mark those occasions. The resulting photographs demonstrate their personal wartime achievements by displaying the additional uniform chevrons, bars or stripes and other qualification badges that signified their advancement (Figs 130 and 131).

When service personnel were serving overseas, maintaining contact with family at home was very important. A soldier might visit a local photographic studio on arrival in, say, North Africa or Italy and post the image back to Britain, to indicate where he was now posted. Exchanging letters and photographs was especially popular at Christmas time when relatives would be acutely aware of the absence of their loved ones. A photographic portrait of the serviceman or woman might be inserted into a folding card printed with a seasonal message or set into a specially designed local postcard bearing the message 'Season's Greetings from . . .' (Fig. 132).

**132. Postcard from the Sudan, Christmas 1941.** It was important for servicemen serving overseas to keep in touch with family at home. A photo might be incorporated into a specially printed card at Christmas.

**133. Women's Auxiliary Air Force – 'A' Watch, *c.* 1939–40.** The Women's Auxiliary Air Force, formed in 1939, issued a female uniform, seen far left, that was identical in style to the male uniform but made of softer cloth. These women's belted raincoats suggest that the photo was taken between 1939 and December 1940, as afterwards raincoats were replaced by warmer greatcoats. Their caps carry the brass RAF badge.

## Semi-formal Group Scenes

As during the previous war, many group scenes of military personnel and members of other wartime organisations, taken by professional photographers in Britain or overseas, survive for the Second World War. These depict family members posing in formation along with their colleagues, wearing uniform relevant to their role and the season and may convey powerfully the spirit of camaraderie that many later remembered as one of the most positive aspects of the war (Figs 133–5). Sometimes these group photographs have been annotated by the family member in the scene, explaining their subject and perhaps the location and the date. Diverse and fascinating, such images may, for example, reveal something of wartime conditions (Fig. 134) or perhaps a special role within the regiment (Fig. 135).

## Amateur Snapshots

Unlike in 1914, amateur photography was firmly established and widespread by the time war erupted for a second time in 1939: between the two world

**134. Royal Army Ordnance Corps workshop, Malta, 1943.** Relatives on active service abroad dressed in more relaxed light khaki uniforms made of cooler material. Only one man here wears battle dress and several mechanics wear one-piece overalls. The bullet-ridden doors behind the group reveal the severity of the attacks made on Malta during its three-year siege. Local children are also in the scene.

**135. Infantry Corps of Drums, 1941–2.** These soldiers wear the inconvenient khaki side cap that was worn until late 1943. No cap badge is visible to identify the regiment, nor is their slip-on shoulder strap badge denoting their regiment readable. Clearly, they served with a Corps of Drums, which were unique to infantry regiments and brass drum badges are visible on their sleeves.

wars many individuals and families had acquired personal photographic equipment and numerous servicemen took a portable camera to war with them. In their 1940 catalogue, Ensign, then the largest British camera manufacturer, seized the opportunity to promote their well-established Ensign Midget camera to the troops, declaring it to be: 'A remarkable war time camera . . . It goes into a tunic pocket with room to spare.' Officially, the troops were forbidden to photograph certain subjects, including German POWs, Allied or

**136. Inside the tent at Khartoum,** *c.* **1940–2.** Many soldiers brought cameras away with them during Second World War and recorded daily life in a military camp. This evocative snapshot of a Royal Army Ordnance Corps tent companion writing home was taken in Khartoum during the North African campaign.

**137. Amateur snapshot taken at home, early 1940.** The difference between First and Second World War uniforms is clear here as this soldier wears the battledress uniform introduced in 1939, including the distinctive short blouse fastened at the waist. This was a 'departure' photograph taken early in 1940: as the war progressed, sleeves would become adorned with cloth insignia.

**138. Amateur snapshot, dated August 1944.** These chums belonged to the Auxiliary Territorial Service, formed in 1938. The women's jackets bore brass Auxiliary Territorial Service shoulder titles and they often wore the cap or collar badge of the units with which they worked. Some Auxiliary Territorial Service members wore more practical battledress with trousers.

enemy military vehicles and equipment, but casual scenes shot around the camp and when off duty were common and provide a unique glimpse of military life (Fig. 136). Large numbers of snapshots were taken in Britain too, during the war. For example, the 'departure' photograph that during the First World War was usually formally set in a professional studio was more likely to take the form of a snapshot in the garden at home (Fig. 137). Friends in military units based in Britain or at home on leave might also take impromptu photographs of one another as personal mementoes of their war (Fig. 138).

## Second World War Wedding Photographs

As we saw in Chapter 10, weddings continued to take place throughout the Second World War and wartime wedding photographs are surprisingly diverse. Photographic evidence suggests that initially conventional 'white' weddings were fairly common: despite (or possibly because of) the war and the growing uniformity of civilian dress, many brides were determined that

**139. Second World War wedding photograph.** This groom wears his best service dress uniform, reserved for special occasions. Its collar and tie and Sam Browne belt demonstrate his officer status, the stars on his shoulder straps confirming his rank as Lieutenant. Jacket and cap insignia identify him as a Canadian officer of the British Columbia Dragoons which served in Britain.

their wedding day would be special, a memorable occasion to treasure in times of escalating hardship. Often bridal gowns from the late 1930s were loaned by friends or relatives, or, following the introduction of clothes rationing in 1941, families might pool their coupons to buy a new white dress or the material to make one, some bridal dresses being expertly fashioned from parachute silk. As more men joined the armed forces, once again military uniform became the accepted mode of wedding attire for bridegrooms (Fig. 139). Increasing numbers of young single women also entered the services, often meeting and marrying fellow servicemen, so that both bride and groom might be pictured in a photograph proudly wearing military uniform on their wedding day.

The presence in Britain of soldiers from around the world led to many international courtships and marriages, like the wedding featured here, between a local girl and Canadian officer (Fig. 139). Sometimes weddings between British women and servicemen from overseas were arranged at short notice, if, for example, the prospective groom had been posted back home, or elsewhere in the world. Brides and their families did not always have the time to organise a formal white wedding or the resources for one – nor were costly, frivolous occasions deemed very appropriate as during the course of the war Britain became gripped by a growing mood of austerity. Consequently, family photographs demonstrate how many civilian brides were married in a smart Utility style knee-length suit or dress, a floral spray or neat posy, attractive waved hairstyle and a stylish hat the most glamorous elements of the occasion.

## Dating Military Photographs and Identifying Uniforms

Images of ancestors and relatives in uniform dominate collections of photographs originating during and immediately after the First and Second World Wars. Of course, some of our forebears had long-term careers in the army, Royal Navy, merchant navy or the air force and may well have been photographed in uniform during peace time, as seen for example in Fig. 147, but in many cases it was the circumstances of war that led to adoption of a uniform. It may be possible to date a military photograph very approximately from the photographic format: for example, if it is presented on a postcard mount, then it must date from between 1902 and around 1950 – a time period that, however, encompasses both world wars. Some of us can distinguish in a general way between photographs exhibiting the standard Great War 1908 pattern army uniform and the battledress of the Second World War, introduced in 1939; however, establishing a precise date that may help to identify firmly an unnamed family member and confirm when they volunteered or were conscripted requires a trained eye. Uniform garment styles can help with close dating: for example, during the Second World War the early battledress blouse gave way in 1940 to the economy battledress, tailored without pleats or button coverings. However, uniforms display many other features including headgear, badges, insignia and equipment that all have their own history and a specific meaning: when identified, a particular cap badge, shoulder title, button design, cloth sleeve badge or gas-mask style can not only help with dating an image, but will usually demonstrate the regiment, rank and role of the wearer. These details are fascinating to discover and will reveal a great deal about a family member's wartime activities.

Explanation of hundreds of different First and Second World War uniforms is well beyond the scope of this book. Like fashion history, acquiring such knowledge can take many years, but some useful books have been published about uniform identification and dating military photographs: these are listed in the Sources section. Fortunately, the two world wars and the uniforms that evolved are of great interest today and there are many military experts ranging from museum curators to private collectors with considerable expertise and access to the necessary resources. Family historians might consider submitting queries to the Imperial War Museum or National Army Museum in London, the RAF Museum or the National Maritime Museum: the remit of their curators includes handling inquiries from the general public, although this is not generally a major priority among their many responsibilities. Otherwise, it may be worth contacting any of the family history magazines that feature a regular readers' military photo dating column, written by their resident expert. There are also various private consultants who provide a professional military photograph dating and identification service. For example, Jon Mills, author and independent military specialist, has helped enormously with the preparation of this chapter, by providing photographs and all of the details for the captions and parts of the text: his contact details are in the Sources section, while other military experts may be found by searching online.

## Wartime Resources

A great deal of surviving historical material relating to the two world wars is available to view in museums and on websites. Both physical and online image collections may well include photographs that portray family members, or that link more generally to the conflicts in which they were involved.

2014 is the centenary of the outbreak of the First World War and numerous commemorative events and projects will be focusing on the war and making more material accessible than ever before. In particular, to mark the centenary, the Imperial War Museum has recently redeveloped its First World War galleries and has also launched a special website, First World War Centenary, 1914–1918, which aims to highlight centenary events and resources from across the globe: www.1914.org. The First World War Centenary Partnership, led by the IWM, is a network of around 1,000 (at time of going to print) local, regional, national and international cultural and educational organisations that will be presenting a programme of events, activities and digital platforms to enable millions across the world to discover more about life during the First World War. One particularly noteworthy project is the interactive digital platform 'Lives of the First World War', which invites family historians and other members of the public to share their family photographs, stories and memorabilia online, to help create a collective record of earlier generations' experiences of the Great War – www.1914.org/news/new-digital-centenary-project-lives-of-the-first-world-war.

While centenary related First World War world-wide, national and local projects and events will extend over the period 2014–18, additional resources relating to both the First and Second World War are becoming available at an impressive rate. In recent years a number of organisations have received substantial Heritage Lottery Funding grants towards projects that aim to make more wartime records and personal memoirs accessible to the general public. These include 'The Story of the North East's Lumber Jills' project based in Chopwell Wood near Gateshead and the Wartime Memories 'Life on the Home Front' project in Stockton-on-Tees – to name but two. In addition, many district archives, libraries and record offices have in their collections local photographs that originated during the two world wars, which may or may not have been digitised and uploaded onto their website: commonly, these include images of the temporary military hospitals that were set up in their area during the First World War, or photographs of the workforce of local munitions factories: such scenes may well include family members who were wounded during the war or who helped to run essential industries. By keeping abreast of the various collections, websites and projects relating to the First and Second World Wars, it is becoming increasingly easy to date and successfully investigate precious family wartime photographs. This is an ideal time to research these images and even become involved in recording our wartime heritage.

# Chapter 13

# LOCAL CONNECTIONS

S ome of the photographs in our archives demonstrate particularly strong connections between family history and local history: in many ways the two are inextricably linked. If ancestors lived, worked and played in a particular hamlet or village, town or city for decades, even generations, then over the years the development of their district will have significantly influenced their lives, while they in turn may well have made a major impact in the locality, perhaps a lasting contribution to their physical environment or active involvement in the social, economic and cultural life of their community. Therefore, using local resources can be invaluable when researching a family's past and, equally, private family records can add an important dimension to the wider history of a particular geographical location.

## School Photographs

A number of families have kept old school photographs, evocative images that portray youthful family members and other children from the neighbourhood among whom they spent their early years. Prestigious schools and academies like Harrow and Eton College employed professional photographers to photograph their pupils as early as the mid-nineteenth century, but official school photography for the wider population only developed after the passing of the 1870 Elementary Education Act, which led to larger numbers of children from ordinary backgrounds attending local schools. Regular photographer visits to local day schools were also encouraged by the technical advances of the 1880s which facilitated work away from the studio. These developments mean that the vast majority of school photographs passed down through families date from the 1880s onwards.

School children were usually photographed in their class groups or perhaps two classes combined, carefully positioned so that each small face was visible (Figs 69 and 140). Typically, in early photographs the children are lined up in rows outside in the playground, the group sometimes flanked by the head teacher and their class teacher, although views taken inside the schoolroom began to appear during the early twentieth century. In many school photographs a child in the centre holds a slate stating the school, class and sometimes the year, as seen in both Figs 69 and 140: these details were intended

**140. St Nicolas's School, Portslade, East Sussex, 1928.** This is a typical school photograph, the children lined up outside in the playground. It is firmly dated and identified, although the girls' bobbed hairstyles and clothing of all of the children would in any case suggest a 1920s date.

to help the photographer later on when developing and sorting the prints, but are very useful for family historians, for confirmation of the school's name and a date can aid identification of an unknown family member. However, if a school photograph is not labelled in this way, the image needs to be dated and further research undertaken, to find out more. It should be possible to establish an approximate time frame from the appearance of the children and, especially, any adults in the picture, whose styles of dress may be easier to pinpoint than juvenile clothing. By the early twentieth century a recognisable uniform was developing for older pupils, although elementary school children often wore their ordinary clothes to school, simply being told to 'come clean' for the photographer's visit. See Chapter 5 for tips on dating girls' and boys' dress.

Another potential method of dating school photographs, and one that can work well alongside dating the fashions, is to try to establish the operational dates of the studio named on the mount, if applicable. The photographer may have been a representative from a nearby commercial studio, although some companies specialised in academic portraiture, using a franchise system or employing country wide agents to visit schools in their local areas, like George Watkins Holden, manager of the Elementary Schools Photographing Company, whose operations extended throughout Britain. A reasonable date range for a school photograph may narrow down the possibilities when attempting to identify the school, and if the institution still exists it is well worth making contact: some schools maintain historical archives including records of past pupils and may even have preserved dated copies of their official school photographs, labelled with the names of the students in the scene. However, sometimes school records have been deposited with the record office for the relevant area, especially if the school has closed down, so local archives and record offices can provide another line of inquiry.

## Local Work Images

As we saw in Chapter 11, sometimes photographs picture ancestors and relatives at work or wearing special occupational dress. Work-related images sometimes demonstrate graphically how our forebears engaged with the industry and commerce of their particular locality – photographs taken by

**141. Duck-plucking at Chinnor, South Oxfordshire, *c.* 1904–9.** The famous white Aylesbury duck was farmed in Aylesbury, Buckinghamshire and in surrounding villages from the 1700s. Many ancestors and relatives from the area worked in this industry until its decline during the early–mid-twentieth century.

**142. The Bath Arms, Minsterley, Shropshire, 1880s.** Public houses and the publicans who ran them were at the centre of the local community. This scene depicts a proprietor and her daughters with their 'regulars' outside the pub that was the family's home and business for several generations.

itinerant photographers, by representatives from local studios hired by an employer to photograph the labour force or by an amateur photographer. As these can reveal, some forebears' occupations were closely linked to the local economy: for example, they may have lived in a geographical area famed for a particular industry or product and followed that line of work (Fig. 141), or perhaps they numbered among the staff of a large company that employed many local inhabitants. Past family members may have provided an essential service, as a policeman, fireman, doctor, postman or bus or tram driver, becoming a familiar friendly figure to many in their community. Some will have been small tradesmen or craftsmen, supplying their neighbourhood with essential items – foodstuffs, clothing, household goods and work equipment. Those who ran such businesses or who worked, for example, in high-street shops or tearooms, or who ran a public house, perhaps served a local clientele for many years and would have been well acquainted with their regular customers and perhaps became prominent members of the local community

**143(a). Guard's outfitters and drapers, Romsey, Hampshire, *c*. 1900.** The relative who took this photograph served as a sales assistant at Guard's outfitters between 1900 and 1946. The shop was in operation by 1891 and only closed in the 1950s. The proprietor, Henry Guard, was Mayor of Romsey in 1897.

**143(b). Inside Guard's outfitters, *c*. 1900.** Early interior views of the workplace are fascinating images. Clothing shop assistants were expected to dress smartly and this staff member, who served at Guards for most of his working life, wears a three-piece lounge suit with high starched shirt collar.

(Figs 142 and 143). Occasionally, an ancestor held a position that gained them a highly visible public profile in their locality (Fig. 144). Even humble ancestors and relatives who played relatively low-key roles, for example as farm labourers or builders, may have helped to shape the landscape or the local streets around them (Fig. 145).

Family photographs of such scenes often connect closely with local documentary records and consulting printed sources can often shed further light on these images or bring them to life, adding some of the background detail that can't be expressed in a picture. Tradesmen, craftsmen, shopkeepers and others running businesses may well have advertised in the local press or in district trade directories – publications that may explain more about their operations. Public houses and publican forebears frequently featured in newspaper reports, and other family members may also have been mentioned in the local news, perhaps in an obituary commemorating their service to the

**144(a). Southampton scene, 1924.** Some family members held high-profile positions in their locality. This ancestor, wearing a white motoring coat, drove the first chauffeured car in Southampton; his many passengers included Edward, Prince of Wales on his visit to the town in 1924.

community (Fig. 144(b)). If their position was deemed important, they may even be mentioned in a book written during their lifetime or in a later local history publication. It is well worth seeking out local books and articles relevant to past generations: these may even include other photographs of family members in addition to the images preserved at home. Many villages and towns now run their own community websites, too: these often include pages relating to the history of the area and display vintage photographs submitted by local residents.

If an ancestor or relative worked for a major local company or for a regional branch of a well-known chain, it may well be possible to find out more about their working lives and perhaps discover further photographs. Some companies, past and present, run websites with interesting history sections or host virtual museums, for example, Marks & Spencer – www.marksintime.marksandspencer.com – and Woolworths – www.woolworthsmuseum.co.uk. Invariably, such sites display historic photographs and may also itemise the kinds of company records that survive and are available for researchers to consult. If, for instance, a company produced a regular staff newsletter, journal or magazine this will probably feature reports of staff social events, employees' promotions, marriages, retirement and so on, along with relevant photographs. In the case of businesses that no longer exist or where, for example, the collection is of special importance, the records and any surviving memorabilia may have been deposited with the district archive, record office, museum or even the main university for the area, so, again, these local repositories can be an invaluable source of information. If earlier generations worked in an area where a particular industry or trade dominated the local economy, the town, city or county museum is almost certain to have collected material of specific

**HE DROVE ROYALTY**

# Soton's former civic chauffeur dies aged 76

THE death has been announced of Mr. Charles Tucker, Kingston-road, Freemantle, Southampton, at the age of 76. Mr Tucker was for about 25 years Mayor's chauffeur in the town.

He first became the Mayor chauffeur during the late Alderman Sir Sidney Kimber's mayoralty in 1918 and 1919. During that time the first mayoral car was bought and Sir Sidney appointed Mr. Tucker as Mayor chauffeur.

Charlie Tucker, as everyone knew him, retired in 1943 and in 1944 he was presented with a set of four pipes, a cheque, and an illuminated address from the surviving Mayors under whom he had served.

From the time of his appointment until his retirement Mr Tucker had driven 23 Mayors.

He joined the Royal Marines as a drummer boy in 1894 and it was in 1908, when he bought himself out of the Service, that he became a chauffeur.

While he was Mayor's chauffeur Mr. Tucker had driven many members of the Royal Family and his passengers also included Sir Winston and Lady Churchill.

He leaves a widow, three sons and a daughter.

**144(b). Newspaper obituary, *Southampton Echo*, 1955.** This ancestor's long career as civic chauffeur to twenty-three Mayors of Southampton and his brush with royalty were recorded in his obituary in the local newspaper. He is also mentioned in the autobiography of one of the local Mayors.

relevance. There may even be a specialist museum in the area dedicated to a significant local occupation such as lace-making, brewing, mining or fishing: photographs in the collection might portray or link directly to past family members; at the very least, they will provide an insight into their working

**145. Amateur snapshot, dated 1949.** A note on the back of this snapshot identifies these workmen as plumbers working on the post-war reconstruction of London County Council flats in Shoreditch.

lives. Always check the museum websites to see what is available to view online or whether it is worth making arrangements to visit in person to study the collections.

## Local Clubs and Teams

Many past family members belonged to local sports teams, church or social clubs, Women's Institute branches, Masonic Lodges or to other societies and organisations that enabled them to socialise with others in the neighbourhood and pursue common interests. The various types of groups to which our forebears may have belonged are numerous and cannot all be covered here, although sport is a good example of a popular activity that drew members of the community together, could arouse lively local interest and might even have helped to define a village, town or city if a local team played against competing teams and gained a wider reputation. In Chapter 11 we considered the kinds of sporting photographs that might occur in a family picture collection: some of these will be official team photographs, taken perhaps at the start of a new sporting season or at the end, if the team won the league cup. Sometimes these images are not labelled, but many early football team photographs, for example, are firmly identified, the name of the club and the year either stated at the bottom of the picture or written on the ball (Fig. 146). In some instances each player is named too, so we may be fortunate in knowing exactly where and when the photograph originated and which sporting ancestor is pictured in the group.

As mentioned earlier, many local sports clubs evolved in the later nineteenth and early twentieth centuries and may well still exist, offering sporting and social facilities to today's generation. Some clubs run official websites and display a historical timeline, honours lists and other information, as well as photographs of teams and prominent players from the past. If it is known or suspected where a family member played football, cricket, bowls, hockey or another sport, the relevant club website may give the contact details

**146. Brighton & Hove Albion football team, 1911.** If past family members were involved with a local sports club they may appear in official team photographs. Clubs that have survived may well keep old photographs and records of past players: some, like the 'Seagulls' pictured below, run a museum.

of someone within their organisation who can respond to a membership or photographic query. Major sports clubs like Wimbledon Lawn Tennis Club and city football clubs such as Liverpool FC and Arsenal also have museums at their grounds or elsewhere, and their staff should be able to reply directly to queries. In addition, details of local sporting events have always been enthusiastically reported in the press, the sports pages of local newspapers usually one of their key features. Many of today's principal regional newspapers keep an archive of their past newspaper reports, including photographs, and will usually respond to inquiries from the general public.

## Local Resources

In general, local newspapers can provide one of the best sources of information about goings-on in the geographical area that they cover. Some have even published pictorial books about local people, places and events based on their archives of old press photographs, which may date back to the nineteenth century. Many regional newspapers also feature a regular 'Nostalgia', 'Past in Pictures' or similar column, resurrecting images from their archives to demonstrate aspects of local life in the past, often inviting readers to submit their own family photographs. This can be a great way of sharing and discussing inherited photographs that have a regional slant, whether the image represents an old school photograph, a works charabanc outing, a seaside 'walking picture' or an unidentified sports team. If, for example, we know or believe that a particular photograph was taken in the Manchester area, but can't date or positively identify the scene, it is worth submitting it to local newspapers covering the city and its environs, to compare with photographic records in their archives, and/or to feature in their local history pages: who knows, a knowledgeable reader may know the answer; they may even have an identical copy of a group photograph in their own family collection, handed down by their ancestors.

In particular, we should not forget the extensive resources offered by local libraries, record offices and archives and museum facilities such as local history study centres for the geographical area(s) under investigation: these organisations generally keep copies of local newspapers, trade directories, sometimes the district's school records, and any amount of primary and secondary historical material relating to the area and its inhabitants. Although it may be necessary to visit an archive or library in person, many public photograph collections are now accessible online and more images are being digitised all the time. Local authorities that have uploaded historic photographs of the region onto searchable websites include Leeds, whose photographic archive can be viewed at www.leodis.net, Staffordshire: www.staffspasttrack. org.uk, and Lincolnshire: www.lincstothepast.com. There are many more examples, so be sure to check whether there are any online photographic resources covering the cities or counties where earlier generations of the family lived. Some local history societies also run websites displaying information, even photographs that may be of potential interest to family historians. The website Local History Online features a directory of over 1,000 local history and associated societies: www.local-history.co.uk/Groups/index.html. Never has there been a better time to tap into a wide range of resources when investigating family photographs and share knowledge across the different historical disciplines.

# Chapter 14

# FOREIGN LOCATIONS

Although holidaying abroad has been a relatively recent development
for many families, there can be few of us without at least one foreign
family connection dating back to a time before travel overseas became
a regular occurrence. Many private picture collections include photographs
that originated outside Britain and tell of lives and experiences beyond these
shores.

How many and what kinds of foreign photographs we have inherited can
depend on various factors including world-wide developments, individual
occupations and family circumstances. It was mainly our affluent (or
adventurous) predecessors who journeyed abroad for pleasure before the mid-
twentieth century, although we should remember that some of our ordinary
ancestors and relatives may have ventured overseas with their job: for
example, perhaps they were personal companions, ladies' maids, governesses,
nannies, valets or other trusted servants accompanying prosperous families
who travelled or resided abroad; or Royal Navy or merchant navy sailors who
spent much of their lives at sea, resting in different ports or being posted to
foreign naval bases (Fig. 147). Many of our forebears tried their hand at
mining or farming in the United States, Canada, Australia or New Zealand
(Fig. 148) or took their trade or profession to newly colonised areas of the
world where support industries and facilities were needed in the developing
settlements. Industrial and economic expansion created many overseas
business opportunities during the nineteenth century and different
destinations became popular at different points in time: for instance, we find
a significant number of ancestors working in South America by the late
nineteenth century, in roles as diverse as timber merchants, railway engineers
and cattle ranchers (Fig. 149). Naturally, countries that were part of the British
Empire, or numbered among its colonies or dominions had established ex-pat
communities that included military personnel, civil servants, missionaries,
tradesmen and their families, so, for example, a number of us have family
members who were born or served in India (Fig. 150). Additionally, many of
our twentieth-century forebears met and perhaps married foreign nationals
during the Second World War.

191

**147. Studio portrait, Malta, 1880s.** Some of our forebears worked abroad and may have visited professional photography studios overseas. This Royal Navy ancestor, dressed in the sailor's white trousers and straw hat worn in hot climates, was stationed at the British naval base in Malta.

**148. Amateur snapshot, Deer Creek Ranch, Saskatchewan, 1912.** This relaxed scene shows relatives taking a lunch break after a morning's work on their Canadian farm. They wear casual outdoor clothes with hats and veils as protection from the sun.

Photographs taken abroad may either be formal studio portraits or casual outdoor snapshots, reflecting the usual mix of images that occur in family picture collections. Commercial photography progressed at a similar rate globally – or at least throughout the developed world, studios becoming established wherever there was popular demand. Therefore, we find professional portrait photography being practised from the mid-nineteenth century onwards in cities as far apart as Calcutta, Buenos Aires, Dublin, Melbourne, Paris, Boston, Cairo and Johannesburg. To some extent photographers adopted new processes and formats more or less simultaneously: in particular the *carte de visite* print became fashionable virtually everywhere during the 1860s, although the humble tintype photograph was popular in the United States much earlier than in Britain and was produced there in far greater numbers. In general, card-mounted prints used similar styles of mounts with comparable designs wherever commercial studios operated, the main differences being the location. Theoretically, it may be possible to discover more about the photographer whose name and address are printed on a foreign mount, although online information is not always available: databases and indexes covering photographers working overseas do exist but may be less comprehensive than their British equivalents. As with

**149. Amateur snapshot, *El Divisorio* Estancia, Argentina, 1886.** South America offered many lucrative opportunities for enterprising Britons in the late nineteenth century. This early amateur snapshot taken by a family member depicts ancestors who ran a cattle ranch enjoying a picnic in the bush.

British photographers, it is recommended that researchers always conduct a general Google search for foreign photographers and studios, to see exactly what information is available and whether a local organisation such as a museum or library may be able to offer further advice.

Victorian and Edwardian ancestors often visited a foreign studio when abroad, either to acquire a photographic travel souvenir, especially if their stay was temporary, or to mark the usual personal and family occasions if they were long-term residents. Generally, the composition of portraits taken overseas followed familiar conventions: for instance, the head and shoulders vignette portrait was equally fashionable in Britain and India during the 1890s (Fig. 150). Studio settings were also broadly comparable internationally, although sometimes a local scene depicting a harbour, palm trees or mountains is painted on the backcloth, reinforcing the foreign location (Fig. 121). Unless they wore an occupational or military uniform, usually visitors to the studio wore their regular fashionable dress: by the mid–late nineteenth century Western-style dress was widely worn throughout the developed world, although there might be regional variations and we may notice minor differences, such as a preference for lightweight, pale-coloured garments and

CALC

**150. Studio portrait, Calcutta, India, 1890s.** Many families have connections to India dating back to the days of the British Raj, or perhaps even earlier. The head and shoulders vignette composition and this ancestor's appearance dates this photograph to the 1890s.

lower shirt collars being worn by European men in hot climates (Fig. 150). Some family photographs originating overseas will be casual snapshots: occasionally a late-nineteenth-century snapshot taken by an early amateur photographer may occur (Fig. 149), although most will date from the twentieth century (Fig. 148). Set outdoors, these scenes from around the world portray family members in their local surroundings and offer a glimpse of everyday experiences abroad that were perhaps very different to their contemporaries' lifestyles in Britain. Such images also include wartime snapshots, especially from the Second World War when many men were stationed abroad and recorded military life overseas using their personal cameras, as discussed in Chapter 12.

Photographs taken abroad, whether formal studio portraits or amateur snapshots, might be sent home as a way for emigrants to keep in touch with relatives; otherwise they may have been brought back if and when the family member(s) returned to Britain. Sometimes images remained overseas with the emigrants' descendants but are now being reconnected by family historians with shared roots communicating across countries or continents: this is becoming increasingly common as photographs are uploaded onto global genealogy websites such as Ancestry and Findmypast. Often we are already aware that past family members emigrated or travelled abroad, although sometimes a foreign photograph can be something of a mystery and needs further investigation. Records that can be used to track down forebears' movements include ships' passenger lists, which can be viewed on the Ancestry and Findmypast websites. Passports were not a legal requirement for travelling across borders until the First World War, although sometimes passports were issued under special circumstances during the nineteenth century and details of these may found at The National Archives. First World War or post-war passport photographs sometimes occur in the family picture collection – clear head and shoulders portraits against a blank background, similar to today's standard passport photographs (Fig. 151).

**151. Passport photograph, mid–late 1920s.** Passports first became a legal requirement during the First World War. From then onwards, official passport photographs may feature in the family collection.

*Part Four*

# LOOKING AFTER FAMILY PHOTOGRAPHS

# *Chapter 15*

# PRESERVING OLD PHOTOGRAPHS

Many of the family photographs in today's collections have survived for well over a century, while the very earliest examples – daguerreotypes – could be 170 years old. This is an impressive life span, but, inevitably, such vulnerable artefacts deteriorate over time due to the nature of the materials used and because of shifts in environmental factors. The continuing survival of our precious photographic heirlooms throughout and beyond the twenty-first century depends upon protecting them from damaging external factors and on responsible handling, storage and display.

## Caring for Photographs

Photographs may seem rather ordinary items but they can be complex objects and often consist of several layers, each containing different substances that react to outside influences in various ways. Consequently, some types of photograph deterioration are, unfortunately, untreatable; so the most helpful advice is to try to prevent common problems occurring in the first place. The potential causes of damage and deterioration to photographs are: high temperatures, which hasten fading and tarnishing; exposure to light, especially bright sunlight, which causes fading; damp conditions, which can produce mould or discolouration; very dry conditions, which cause brittleness and cracking; poor quality or unsuitable storage, framing and mounting methods which may emit pollutants, causing fading, discolouration and tarnishing and can also create physical damage such as tears and creases; and staining from sticky adhesive tapes and album pages. In addition, some photographs are at risk from insect attack such as silverfish, woodworm, booklice and carpet beetle; handling causes further deterioration as dirt can scratch vulnerable surfaces, while fingers may leave print marks and damaging moisture from the skin. It is a fact that many old photographs are taken out and handled frequently, because they are so portable and because we enjoy looking at them and showing them to others, but there are various methods of preventing and reducing deterioration.

## Storage

Photographs should be stored in a cool place where conditions are neither very damp nor very dry: therefore, they should not be kept in damp basements or garages, or in stuffy, un-insulated lofts. Preferably, there should be no significant fluctuations, a stable environment with a relative humidity within the range 30–40 per cent being ideal. It is important to store and organise photographs using products of recognised archival quality (see below). Original daguerreotype and ambrotype frames and cases and old albums should be regarded as integral to the photographs they contain and in these instances it is important to keep the whole artefact intact. If any elements of the picture have a problem, for example if a case is broken, this should be repaired by a professional conservator who will use processes geared towards maintaining the integrity of the photograph in its original context.

## Display

Although it is tempting to exhibit old family photographs where they can be seen, try to avoid displaying them at high light levels, or for long periods of time. Ultraviolet filtering glass helps to protect photographs during periods of light exposure. Any framing materials should also be of high quality.

## Handling

Try to keep handling of original photographs to a minimum, but if it is necessary, make sure that hands are clean and dry or, ideally, wear lint-free cotton researchers' gloves. Hold photographs by their edges and use a supporting base such as stiff paper or card to move fragile photographs. Scanning photographs once, then storing them suitably, working instead from printed copies or digital images on the computer, saves regular handling of the fragile originals.

For more detailed information about looking after photographs, visit the website of the Institute of Conservation: www.icon.org.uk. If in any doubt at all about the preservation or repair of old photographs in any format, advice from a professional conservator is always recommended: the aim of photograph conservation is to reverse damage if at all possible, and to ensure that future deterioration is reduced to a minimum. The ICON website also includes a register of qualified conservators.

## Conservation Quality Archival Storage Materials

Public museums, art galleries and archives always preserve their photographs and other important items such as historical documents and antique books in purpose-designed conservation quality storage systems. These provide fragile and potentially vulnerable objects with physical support and protection against permanent damage and decay in an acid-free environment. The kinds of products used by institutions are also commercially available to the general public and so it is easy to take good care of family pictures and other important

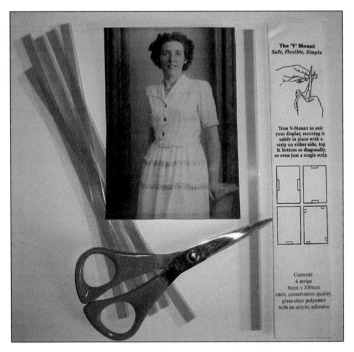

**152. Archival quality photograph accessories.** These professional clear polyester 'V' mounting strips, more convenient than glue or tape, are acid-free and therefore ideal for safely mounting and displaying old photos. Many conservation quality products suitable for photographs are widely available.

keepsakes in a professional manner. This applies not only to historical material but also to more recent photographs and family papers that need to be preserved for future generations.

The archival products available offer many different storage and display solutions, including acid-free boxes of varying shapes and sizes, ring binder systems, album pages, folders, envelopes, pockets, sleeves and even CD cases. Especially useful for convenient handling and viewing of photographs of different sizes are transparent inert polyester pockets which don't contain harmful chemicals and are safe for long-term storage. Other accessories include researchers' lint-free cotton gloves, pH neutral pens and mounting products such as acid-free paper, mount strips and adhesive. These and other conservation materials are available from specialist companies who can advise about the best products to use for particular requirements, and from many general genealogical suppliers (Fig. 152). Look online or in the advertising sections of genealogy magazines: some companies also attend local family history events.

# SOURCES

**Further Reading**
**History of Photography and Guides to Photographic Formats**
Coe, Brian, *The Birth of Photography*, Ash & Grant, 1976
Coe, Brian and Gates, Paul, *The Snapshot Photograph: The Rise of Popular Photography, 1888–1939*, Ash & Grant, 1977
Cox, Paul and Forbes, Heather, *Beautiful Ambrotypes*, Travelling Light, 1989
Falconer, John and Hide, Louise, *Points of View: Capturing the 19th century in Photographs*, British Library, 2009
Gernsheim, Helmut and Alison, *The History of Photography*, Thames & Hudson, 1969
Hannavy, John, *Victorian Photographers at Work*, Shire, 1997
Linkman, Audrey, *The Victorians: Photographic Portraits*, Tauris Parke, 1993
Pols, Robert, *My Ancestor was a Studio Photographer*, Society of Genealogists, 2011
Wichard, Robin and Carol, *Victorian Cartes-de-visite*, Shire, 1999

**Selected Publications on Regional Photographers**
A more extensive list is included in *My Ancestor was a Studio Photographer* by Robert Pols – see above.

**Berkshire**
Cannon, P, *A Directory of photographers: Newbury and district 1854–1945*, Newbury District Museum, 1997
**Channel Islands**
Mayne, Richard and Stevens, Joan, *Jersey Through the Lens*, Phillimore, 1975
**Cornwall**
Thomas, Charles, *Views and likenesses: early photographers and their work in Cornwall and the Isles of Scilly 1839–1870*, Royal Institution of Cornwall, 1988
**Hampshire**
Norgate, Martin, *Directory of Hampshire Photographers 1850–1969*, Hampshire County Council Museums Service, 1995
**Hertfordshire**
Pritchard, Michael and Smith, Bill, *Hertfordshire Photographers 1839–1939*, privately published, Stevenage, 1985
**Lancashire**
Jones, Gillian, *Lancashire Professional Photographers, 1840–1940*, PhotoResearch, 2004
Linkman, Audrey, *Manchester Photographers 1901–1936*, Documentary Photography Archive, 1988
**London/Middlesex**
Pritchard, Michael, *A Directory of London Photographers 1841–1908*, PhotoResearch, 1994
**Northern Ireland**
Maguire, W A, *A Century in Focus: Photography and Photographers in the North of Ireland, 1839–1939*, Blackstaff Press, 2000

**Republic of Ireland**

Chandler, E and Walsh, P, *Through the brass-lidded eye: photography in Ireland 1839–1900*, Guinness Museum, 1989

**Scotland**

McCoo, Don, *Paisley Photographers 1850–1900*, Foulis Archive Press, 1986

Stevenson, Sara and Morrison-Low, A D, *Scottish Photography: A Bibliography 1839–1939*, Salvia Books and Scottish Society for the History of Photography, 1990

**Warwickshire**

Aston, C E John, Hallett, Michael and McKenna, Joseph, *Professional photographers in Birmingham 1842–1914*, RPS Historical Group, 1987

**Wiltshire**

Norgate, Martin, Blades, Judith and Slocombe, Pamela, *Photographers in Wiltshire 1842–1939*, Wiltshire Library & Museum Service, 1985

**Yorkshire**

Adamson, Keith I P, *Photographers in Victorian Doncaster 1842–1900*, Doncaster Museum Service, 1998

Budge, Adrian, *Early Photography in Leeds, 1839–1870*, Leeds Art Galleries, 1981

Murray, Hugh, *Photographs and Photographers of York: The early years 1844–1879*, Yorkshire Architectural and York Archaeological Society, 1988

**Photograph Dating Guides**

Linkman, Audrey, *The Expert Guide to Dating Family Photographs*, Greater Manchester County Record Office, 2000

Pols, Robert, *Dating Nineteenth Century Photographs*, The Alden Press, 2005

Pols, Robert, *Dating Twentieth Century Photographs*, The Alden Press, 2005

Shrimpton, Jayne, *Family Photographs and How to Date Them*, Countryside Books, 2008

Shrimpton, Jayne, *How to Get the Most from Family Pictures*, Society of Genealogists, 2011

**Fashion in Photographs**

The *Fashion in Photographs* series is published by B T Batsford in conjunction with the National Portrait Gallery:

Lambert, Miles, *Fashion in Photographs, 1860–1880*, 1991

Levitt, Sarah, *Fashion in Photographs, 1880–1900*, 1991

Rolley, Katrina, *Fashion in Photographs, 1900–1920*, 1992

Owen, Elizabeth, *Fashion in Photographs, 1920–1940*, 1993

Gernsheim, Alison, *Victorian and Edwardian Fashion: A Photographic Survey*, Dover Publications, 1963

Lansdell, Avril, *Everyday Fashions of the 20th Century*, Shire Books, 1999

Shrimpton, Jayne, *Family Photographs and How to Date Them*, Countryside Books, 2008

Shrimpton, Jayne, *How to Get the Most from Family Pictures*, Society of Genealogists, 2011

**Dress History – General and Specialised**

These highly illustrated books are all written by trained dress historians and are among the best visual guides to the development of fashion and dress.

Blackman, Cally, *One Hundred Years of Menswear*, Laurence King Publishing, 2009

Buck, Anne, *Clothes & the Child: A handbook of children's dress in England 1500–1900*, Ruth Bean, 1996

Byrd, Penelope, *The Male Image: Men's Fashion in England, 1300–1970*, B T Batsford, 1979

Byrde, Penelope, *A Visual History of Costume: The Twentieth Century*, B T Batsford, 1986

Ewing Elizabeth, *History of Children's Costume*, B T Batsford, 1977

Ewing, Elizabeth, *History of 20th Century Fashion*, B T Batsford, 1986

Foster, Vanda, *A Visual History of Costume: The Nineteenth Century*, B T Batsford, 1984

Lansdell, Avril, *Wedding Fashions, 1860–1940*, Shire Publications, 1983

Rose, Clare, *Children's Clothes*, B T Batsford, 1989

Shrimpton, Jayne, *British Working Dress*, Shire Books, 2012

Shrimpton, Jayne, *Fashion in the 1920s*, Shire Books, 2013

Taylor, Lou, *Mourning Dress*, George Allan & Unwin, 1983

## Military Photographs and Uniforms

Mills, Jon, *From Scarlet to Khaki*, Wardens Publishing, 1988 (email: cdwardens@yahoo.co.uk)

Pols, Robert, *Dating Old Army Photographs*, Family History Partnership, 2011

Storey, Neil, *Military Photographs and How to Date Them*, Countryside Books, 2009

## Web Resources
## Regional Photographer Websites and Searchable Photographer Indexes

These online resources vary in their scope and content. Some also provide a history of photography in their respective area(s) and may include biographies of selected local photographers and examples of their work. These listings are correct at time of going to print, but readers should conduct regular searches as data is continually expanding.

### Bristol
Bristol photographers, 1852–1972:
http://www.rogerco.pwp.blueyonder.co.uk/search/bristolphotographers.htm

### Cambridgeshire
Early photographic studios: A–Z directories of photographers in Cambridgeshire, Huntingdonshire, Leicestershire, Norfolk, Northamptonshire, Rutland and Suffolk:
www.early-photographers.org.uk

### Channel Islands
Jersey photographers and studios:
www.jerseyfamilyhistory.co.uk

### Derbyshire
Photographers and photographic studios in Derbyshire:
www.genealogy.rootsweb.ancestry.com/~brett/photos/dbyphotos.html

### Hampshire
Isle of Wight photographers, *c.* 1840–1940:
www.iowphotos.info/

### Huntingdonshire
Early photographic studios: A–Z directories of photographers in Cambridgeshire, Huntingdonshire, Leicestershire, Norfolk, Northamptonshire, Rutland and Suffolk:
www.early-photographers.org.uk

**Isle of Man**
Isle of Man photographers:
www.isle-of-man.com/manxnotebook/tourism/pgrphrs
**Kent**
Photographers in Kent, 1855:
www.kent-opc.org/photographers.html
**Leicestershire**
Early photographic studios: A–Z directories of photographers in Cambridgeshire,
Huntingdonshire, Leicestershire, Norfolk, Northamptonshire, Rutland and Suffolk:
www.early-photographers.org.uk
**London**
Database of nineteenth-century photographers and allied trades in London, 1841–1901:
www.photolondon.org.uk
**Norfolk**
Early photographic studios: A–Z directories of photographers in Cambridgeshire,
Huntingdonshire, Leicestershire, Norfolk, Northamptonshire, Rutland and Suffolk:
www.early-photographers.org.uk
**Rutland**
Early photographic studios: A–Z directories of photographers in Cambridgeshire,
Huntingdonshire, Leicestershire, Norfolk, Northamptonshire, Rutland and Suffolk:
www.early-photographers.org.uk
**Scotland**
History of photography in Edinburgh:
www.edinphoto.org.uk.
Glasgow's Victorian photographers:
www.thelows.madasafish.com/main.htm
**Suffolk**
Early photographic studios: A–Z directories of photographers in Cambridgeshire,
Huntingdonshire, Leicestershire, Norfolk, Northamptonshire, Rutland and Suffolk:
www.early-photographers.org.uk
**Sussex**
Sussex photo history:
www.photohistory-sussex.co.uk/index.htm.
Directory of photographic studios in Brighton and Hove, 1841–1910:
www.spartacus.schoolnet.co.uk/Brighton-Photographers.htm
**Wales**
Victorian professional photographers in Wales, 1850–1925:
www.genuki.org.uk/big/wal/VicPhoto1.html
**Warwickshire**
Victorian photography studios in and around Birmingham and Warwickshire:
www.hunimex.com/warwick/photogs.html

**Professional Photographer/Photography Websites and Photo Dating Services**
Photographers of Great Britain and Ireland, 1840–1940:
www.cartedevisite.co.uk
This important resource covers studio photographs, photographers and their customers.

Studio data is available for many British photographers for a small fee, or visitors can pay to date their card mounts via the photo Dating Wizard.

Index of British portrait and studio photographers, *c.* 1840–1950:
www.earlyphotographers.org.uk
This website provides useful onward links to regional photographer/photography websites. Data can be supplied on individual photographers for a small fee.

www.jayneshrimpton.co.uk
The author's website offers a unique picture (photographs and artworks) dating and analysis service for researchers seeking a professional opinion from a qualified dress historian and experienced portrait specialist. Fees vary according to level of service.

## Major UK Photographic Collections
Many public museums and galleries hold important photographic material of local and national interest. A selection of some of the principal British photograph collections are listed here.
**National Portrait Gallery**
www.npg.org.uk
**National Media Museum, Bradford**
www.nationalmediamuseum.org.uk
**Victoria & Albert Museum, London**
www.vam.ac.uk
**The British Library (Photographically Illustrated Books Collection)**
www.bl.uk
**The National Library of Ireland**
http://www.nli.ie
**Scottish Life Archive, Edinburgh**
www.nms.ac.uk/our_collections/scottish_life_archive.aspx
**Documentary Photography Archive, Manchester**
www.gmcro.co.uk/Photography/DPA/collections.htm

## Further Image Resources and Research Tools
### General Historical Image Websites
www.english-heritage.org.uk
www.imagesofengland.org.uk
www.historypin.com
www.flickr.com

### Selected Occupational Image Sources
**Flickr images**
www.flickr.com/search/?q=occupational+photos
**Museum of English Rural Life, Reading**
www.reading.ac.uk/merl
**Scottish Fisheries Museum**
www.scotfishmuseum.org
**Imperial War Museum**
www.iwm.org.uk

**London Transport Museum**
www.ltmuseum.co.uk
**British Tramway Company Buttons and Badges**
www.birches.plus.com
**The British Postal Museum & Archive**
www.postalheritage.org.uk
**City of London Police Museum**
www.citypolicemuseum.org.uk
**Durham Mining Museum**
www.dmm.org.uk

**Selected Military Image Sources**
**Imperial War Museum**
www.iwm.org.uk
**National Army Museum**
www.nam.ac.uk/online-collection/results.php?searchType=simple&resultsDisplay=list&simpleText=Photographs
**Royal Air Force Museum**
www.rafmuseum.org.uk/research/default/photographs.aspx
**National Maritime Museum**
http://collections.rmg.co.uk/collections.html#!csearch;searchTerm=Photographs

**Listed Buildings**
www.britishlistedbuildings.co.uk

**British Newspaper Archive**
www.britishnewspaperarchive.co.uk

**Trade Directories**
www.historicaldirectories.org

**Postcard Portraits ('Real Photos')**
http://www.playle.com/realphoto/

**Surrey Vintage Vehicle Society**
www.svvs.org

**Ships' Passenger Lists**
www.findmypast.co.uk
www.ancestorsonboard.com
www.ancestry.co.uk

# INDEX